Outrageous
CHESS PROBLEMS

Burt Hochberg

Sterling Publishing Co., Inc.
New York

For Carol

Library of Congress Cataloging-in-Publication Data Available

Edited by Peter Gordon
Diagrams by M-Mate-Chess

2   4   6   8   10   9   7   5   3   1

Published in 2005 by Sterling Publishing Co., Inc.
387 Park Avenue South, New York, NY 10016
© 1999 by Burt Hochberg
Originally published under the title *Chess Braintwisters*
Distributed in Canada by Sterling Publishing
C/o Canadian Manda Group, 165 Dufferin Street
Toronto, Ontario, Canada M6K 3H6
Distributed in Great Britain by Chrysalis Books Group PLC
The Chrysalis Building, Bramley Road, London W10 6SP, England
Distributed in Australia by Capricorn Link (Australia) Pty. Ltd.
P.O. Box 704, Windsor, NSW 2756, Australia

Sterling ISBN 1-4027-1909-4

Contents

What's Going On Here

I am not a problemist. In the three decades that I've been writing about chess and other games, I have created exactly one problem, which appeared in *Chess Life & Review* (now *Chess Life*) in 1976. Here it is: my first and, you will be glad to know, last effort. My purpose in showing it to you is to tell you something about the nature of this book.

How many queens of the same color can you arrange on the board so that no queen attacks any other?

Solution: Sixty-four! Queens of the same color do not attack each other.

Unfair you say? Not at all. If you had read the stipulation carefully and made no assumptions, you might have found the answer easily.

That, in essence, is what this book is about. In it there are some orthodox direct-mate problems, construction tasks, and semi-orthodox helpmates and retractors, but most of the residents here are, shall we say, a little eccentric.

You will see that I like retrograde analysis problems. I also enjoy chess variants such as grid chess, cylinder chess, refusal chess, and losing chess. One variant even features pieces that have had too much to drink (number 82). I especially like joke problems that ignore, not to say flout, not to say stomp on, the Laws of Chess. The rules for each variant are given when appropriate. The solutions, unlike those in every other problem book I've ever seen, explain everything.

It will be helpful in approaching many of these problems to observe the following guidelines:

1. Anything goes.
2. Do not drink and solve.
3. Do not assume anything that is not explicitly stated.
4. Do not assume that the position is legal.
5. Do not assume that it is always White's move.

6. Do not assume that the board is correctly oriented.
7. Do not assume that the Laws of Chess are strictly observed.
8. Do not assume that the composer is playing fair.
9. Do not assume.

For the most part I have selected problems that are, in my opinion, delightful, ingenious, imaginative, provocative, funny, outrageous, thought-provoking, or all of the above. I've stuffed them into sections that I have arranged more or less in order of increasing difficulty, complexity, and weirdness, and I've arranged the problems within each section the same way. You should probably solve them in order, but you don't have to. I have generally preferred positions with few pieces and short solutions, but some will test even the most expert solvers; these are presented more as examples of the composer's art than as puzzles for solving.

This book, though it bears my name, is a compilation of problems created by others. This is where they are traditionally thanked, and I do now thank them all, living and dead, for the great pleasure they have given me. It is my hope and expectation that you will derive as much pleasure from these extraordinary works of the chess imagination as I have.

I want to express my gratitude in particular to John Beasley, Noam D. Elkies, and Adrian Storisteanu, who so generously sent me their creations. Messrs. Beasley and Elkies also sent me compositions by others that they felt might suit the theme of this book, and answered many questions I had about them. Noam Elkies kindly agreed to read the proofs, and corrected a distressing number of errors. It has become a cliché for an author to say that his book would not have been possible without the help of certain individuals, and though as an editor I abhor clichés, there's no getting around it: This book would not have been possible without the help and advice of the above-named composers and other people, notably *Chess Life* editor Glenn Petersen and Jo Anne Fatherly of the U.S. Chess Federation, and it would not have been possible without the encouragement and good counsel of my indefatigable editor, Peter Gordon.

—Burt Hochberg

Things You Should Know

The reader of this book is assumed to be familiar with the essential mechanics of chess: how the pieces move; the rules for castling and en passant captures; the meaning of checkmate, stalemate; and so on. If you are not—if, say, you've never played chess in your life but have been marooned on a desert island with nothing but the clothes on your back and, of all things, this single, solitary book—you should take the Crash Course on Chess that begins on page 113.

There are some terms and conventions, and some unconventional conventions, that apply to many of the problems in this book and that you may not be familiar with even if you've been playing chess all your life. Do yourself a favor: Read these definitions and explanations before attempting to solve the problems, and refer to them whenever you run into one that cannot possibly be solved, you think.

Billiards chess: In this variant, a piece can optionally carom off the side of the board at a right angle to its original direction of movement. A caroming piece can continue to carom until the player decides to stop it or until it either captures an enemy man along its path or runs into a friendly man.

Castling, castle: 1. A special move that may be played once per player in a game, castling is the only time that two pieces of the same color may move on the same turn. Under orthodox rules, the king castles by moving two squares toward a rook on the same rank while the rook moves to the adjacent square on the other side of the king. The king and rook may not have previously moved, the king may not be in check at the time (although it may have been previously checked), and the squares it passes over and lands on may not be under attack. In problems, castling is always allowed unless retrograde analysis proves that it is illegal (by demonstrating that the king or rook has previously moved). See "Legality" and "Retrograde analysis." 2. The noun "castle" is erroneously used by novices who don't know that the piece that looks like a castle turret is called a rook.

Checkless chess: A variant in which check is an illegal move unless it's checkmate. Beware of clever traps where a defense against mate is check but not mate and is therefore not a legal defense.

Checkmate in n moves: The basic stipulation for virtually all orthodox, direct-mate problems. White always moves first (in orthodox problems!). If the stipulation is "White mates in two," White must deliver checkmate on his second move no matter what Black's single defensive move is.

Circe chess: In this variant, named for the goddess who turned Ulysses' men into animals, captured men are immediately returned to the board. A pawn is returned to the second/seventh rank on the file on which it was captured; a piece is returned to its home space of the color square on which it was captured. If a replacement square is occupied, the man is simply captured and removed from play. A capture is illegal if replacing the piece would check the capturing player.

Cook: A fatal flaw that makes a problem unsolvable and unsound. For instance, if a problem requiring mate in four moves actually takes longer or can't be forced at all, or if it can be solved in fewer moves than stipulated, the problem is cooked.

Cylinder chess: A problem variant that imagines the board wrapped around a vertical cylinder so that the leftmost and right-most files (the a-file and the h-file) are contiguous, allowing pieces to move "around the cylinder." A piece may thus end its move where it began. In other forms, the cylinder is horizonal (the first and eighth ranks are contiguous), and sometimes it is, as it were, a double cylinder, both horizontal and vertical, a nightmarish problem variant called an "anchor ring."

Defense: In a problem, one side tries to achieve mate while the other side tries to avoid being mated by putting up the best defense. Generally, White attacks, Black defends. In competitive chess play, a defense is also a system of opening play used by Black, such as the Sicilian Defense.

Direct mate: This is the term problemists use for orthodox problems that require checkmate in a given number of moves against any defense, with White moving first. Helpmates, selfmates, and other varieties fall into a category called unorthodox, heterodox, or "fairy" problems. Many problemists feel that two-move and three-move direct-mate problem themes are played out. Since long-solution problems are usually too difficult for most solvers, constructors are turning to fairy compositions, which offer a wide range of new themes to explore and broad scope for the imagination.

Discovered check or mate: When a man that is standing between a friendly man and the enemy king moves away and thereby allows the friendly piece to attack the king without moving, this is a discovered check or mate. If the moving piece also gives check at the same time, this is called—what else?—double check.

Double-move chess: A rare variant related to Marseillais chess. Each side makes two moves on the same turn with the same piece or two different pieces. The object is to capture the enemy king, but there is no check and a king may move into and out of "check" on the same turn.

Dual: An unintended second solution to a problem. A dual on the first move is a fatal flaw and the composition is unsound. On later moves it's called a "minor" dual—less serious but still a flaw. In some helpmate and selfmate problems, however, and more rarely in direct-mate problems, a double solution is intended by the composer and stated as part of the stipulation. See "Cook."

Dummy: 1. A pawn or piece that does not move, does not capture or give check, and may not be captured. 2. A person who buys books "for Dummies" published by IDG Press.

Endgame study: A composed position that is usually a realistic endgame situation in which the solver is asked to demonstrate a win or a draw. Unlike problems, there is no requirement to give mate and no limit on the number of moves.

En passant: A special capture that each pawn may make once in its life. It must be made at the first opportunity or not at all. When a pawn advances two squares on its first turn, an enemy pawn on its fifth rank and on a file adjacent to the advancing pawn may capture it "in passing," as if it had advanced only one square. In problems, an en passant capture is allowed only if retrograde analysis proves that the opposing pawn must have advanced two squares on the last move. See "Legality" and "Retrograde analysis."

Grid chess: A chess variant that superimposes a grid over the chessboard dividing it into 16 two-by-two sections. Each move must be made to a different section, just as in orthodox chess each move must be made to a different square. Pieces within the same section have no effect on each other.

Helpmate: In orthodox, direct-mate problems, White moves first and must mate Black in a specified number of moves against the best defense. In a helpmate problem, Black moves first. Instead of offering the best defense (as he would if he were trying to avoid being mated), Black makes moves that help White achieve mate in the specified number of moves. In a helpmate in two, for instance, Black moves first, then White, then Black, and finally White gives mate on his second move.

Imitator: A little-explored problem theme. Somewhere on the board the constructor places an imitator, a neutral noncombatant that moves simultaneously and in parallel with every moving piece. A move is illegal if it forces the imitator off the board or into a man of either color.

Key: The first move of a problem solution.

Kriegspiel: In this popular variant, each player has his own board and can see only his own men. Between the players is an umpire with a third board showing the positions of both sides' men. It's a game of logic in which the players attempt to play moves ("tries"), often intentionally impossible ones, in order to deduce the location of opposing men. In the most widely accepted set of rules (there are several versions), if the referee announces that a move is illegal, the player may make further tries until one of them is legal, which he must then play. The umpire announces check by reporting only the direction it comes from. And he announces a capture by naming the square it takes place on, not the pieces involved. The players may speak only to ask the referee whether a pawn capture is possible ("Are there any?" or simply "Any?"). If so, the player must attempt a pawn capture. If it fails, he may try any other move.

Legality: All orthodox problem positions, and positions in most unorthodox forms, must be reachable by a legal, albeit bizarre, sequence of moves. They cannot contain more than 16 men per side, and each promoted piece must be accounted for by a missing pawn. Pawn positions that cannot be reached by normal moves are not allowed. The side not on the move must have had a previous legal move leading to the present position. However, in certain types of construction puzzles, in many unorthodox problems, and particularly in "joke" problems that deliberately flout the Laws of Chess (that is, in a large number of the problems in this book), legality is "a custom more honored in the breach than the observance." When solving a problem where castling or an en passant capture seems possible, the rule is this: Castling is always legal unless it can be proved illegal by retrograde analysis (i.e., by proving that the king or rook has previously moved); en passant is always illegal unless retrograde analysis proves that the other side has just advanced an appropriate pawn two squares.

Losing chess: The object of this popular variant is to force your opponent to capture all your pieces, including the king. There is no check or checkmate. Captures are compulsory.

Men, pieces: Pieces are the king, queen, bishop, knight, and rook. Pawns are pawns. Although the word "pieces" is often used generically for any mixed group, purists prefer "pieces" for pieces, "pawns" for pawns, "men" for a mixed group, and "man" for an unspecified type of unit.

Miniature: A problem with no more than seven men for both sides combined.

Move: An action by a single player. Also, a pair of moves by both players, depending on context. "White mates in three moves" means three moves by White (Black gets to make only two moves). When referring to the score of a game, "moves" means moves by White. For instance, "Hochberg beat Kasparov in 17 moves" means Hochberg made 17 moves, Kasparov 16.

Neutral: A pawn or piece belonging to both sides. A neutral may check either king, and may capture or be captured by a man of either side, including another neutral. A neutral pawn promotes to a neutral piece. White moves a neutral pawn up the board like a White pawn; Black moves it down the board like a Black pawn.

Orthodox: Following all the laws and conventions of chess or chess composition.

Pin: A man that is standing between an enemy piece and a friendly man and is thus blocking the friendly piece from attack is pinned. That is, it can't move without exposing the piece behind it to capture (not always a bad thing). If that piece is the king, however, the pin is "absolute," and the pinned man cannot legally move because it would expose the king to check.

Promotion, underpromotion: A pawn that reaches its eighth rank is required to be promoted. In most cases, a pawn is promoted to the most powerful piece in the army, the queen. But it is often better, for immediate tactical reasons, to "underpromote" to a lesser piece. You will also see in this book various illegal promotions to pieces of the other color, or to kings, neutrals, etc. Just as in real war, soldiers of the lowest rank sometimes switch sides.

Refusal chess: Each player on each turn may refuse the move made by his opponent, who must then offer an alternative. This move may not be refused.

Retract, retractor: A retractor is a type of problem in which you are asked to take back (retract) one or more moves and then carry out a mate in a specified number of "forward" moves (i.e., moves made from the position after the retractions). A typical stipulation is "White and Black retract their last moves, then White mates in one."

Retrograde analysis: The process of proving what the "history" (i.e., the last one or more moves) of a given position must have been. The analysis, which is based on such things as the number of possible captures given the number and positions of the pawns, is used to prove, for instance, whether in the present position castling or en passant is legal. "Retros," as such problems are called, offer probably the greatest scope for the construction of the logical type of chess problem.

Selfmate: In a helpmate, Black moves first and tries to help White give mate. In a selfmate, White moves first and tries to *force* Black to give mate in the specified number of moves.

Series helpmate, series selfmate: Here, one side or the other makes a specified number of non-checking moves, while the other side does not move. At the end of the series, a designated side mates on the move.

Set play: Black moves first in a helpmate. Sometimes the composer provides "set play": a solution that works if it's White's move but doesn't work if it's Black's.

Twins: Two or more closely related problem positions. Sometimes a position is moved to another location on the board with the relative positions of the men unchanged but requiring a different solution. Usually a single man is moved to a new location.

Variant, variation: A variant is a game or problem theme related to chess. Kriegspiel and losing chess, for instance, are variants. A variation is one of several lines of play stemming from a given position, or is part of an opening system (such as the Najdorf Variation of the Sicilian Defense).

13

Algebraic Notation

A simple system is used to record chess moves so that games and positions can be easily reconstructed and played over. It is called algebraic notation. This system has largely replaced the older "descriptive" notation, which is not used in this book and will not be described here.

There are two forms of algebraic notation, "long algebraic" and "abbreviated algebraic." The abbreviated form is used in this book.

The chessboard consists of eight vertical columns, called files, and eight horizontal rows, called ranks (recalling the military origins of chess). The intersections of those rows and columns give the individual squares their names. All references are from the White side of the board and each square has only one name.

The vertical files are lettered from a to h starting at White's left and are called the a-file, the b-file, the c-file, and so on. The horizontal ranks are numbered from 1 to 8 starting at the rank nearest White and are called the first rank, the second rank, the third rank, and so on. The near left corner square is a1, the far right corner square is h8. Each square is mapped on the diagram below.

8	a8	b8	c8	d8	e8	f8	g8	h8
7	a7	b7	c7	d7	e7	f7	g7	h7
6	a6	b6	c6	d6	e6	f6	g6	h6
5	a5	b5	c5	d5	e5	f5	g5	h5
4	a4	b4	c4	d4	e4	f4	g4	h4
3	a3	b3	c3	d3	e3	f3	g3	h3
2	a2	b2	c2	d2	e2	f2	g2	h2
1	a1	b1	c1	d1	e1	f1	g1	h1
	a	b	c	d	e	f	g	h

The pieces are abbreviated K for king, Q for queen, R for rook, B for bishop, and N for knight. A move is recorded by naming the piece that is moving and the square it is moving to. For instance, Be5 means a bishop moves to the square e5. Since only one bishop can move there, the notation is unambiguous. When either of two pieces can move to the same square, the moving piece is more clearly identified. For instance, Rcc2 means the rook on the c-file moves to c2, but Rec2 means the rook on the e-file moves to c2.

A pawn move is usually recorded by naming only the square it moves to. A pawn promotion names the square followed by the = sign and the piece the pawn is promoted to. For instance, d8=Q means a pawn moves to the d8 square and is promoted to a queen.

In this book (but not in every book), a capture is indicated by the letter x between the moving piece and the square. For instance, Bxe5 means a bishop captures on e5. Check is indicated by the symbol + after the move. Re7+ means a rook moves to e7 checking the enemy king.

The moves of a game are numbered in pairs, with White's moves given first (except in helpmate problems, where Black moves first). The first two moves of a game might read: 1 e4 c5 2 Nf3 Nc6, etc. When a move by Black is given without a previous White move (e.g., in the analysis of a position or the continuation of a game score interrupted after a White move), the missing White move is represented by an ellipsis; for instance, "Black should have played 6 ... Be6."

Other symbols used in chess scorekeeping are:

!, a surprisingly good move

!!, a really surprisingly good move

?, a mistake

??, an outright blunder

!?, a risky and probably good move

?!, a risky and probably bad move

?!? (or some similar combination), an incomprehensible move

Orthodox, More or Less

Although this book is dedicated to the proposition that all forms of chess composition are created equal but unorthodox compositions are more equal than others, I am including a small selection of orthodox problems. None of them, however, is *orthodox* orthodox: each one deviates from the norm in a particularly entertaining way.

1.

Most problems ask you to find a checkmate or a win. In keeping with the perverse ideals of this book, we begin with a classic non-mate.

Karl Fabel, *Rätselstunde*, 1952

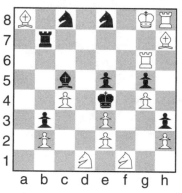

White to move and not mate

2.
Karl Fabel, *Weltspiegel*, 1946

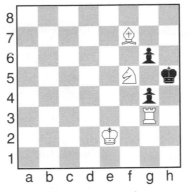

White adds a pawn and mates in 2

3.

Many romantic and fanciful stories are told about Paolo Boi (1528–1598), an interesting character and perhaps the greatest player of the 16th century. One such story, which I have taken the liberty of embroidering a bit since Boi isn't here to contradict me, concerns a game he supposedly played against a mysterious and beautiful woman.

V. Barthe, *Les Cahiers de l'Echiquier Français*, 1936

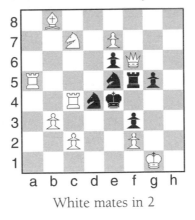

White mates in 2

After a difficult struggle the game reached this position, re-created by Monsieur Barthe, in which Boi announced mate in two. But just as he was about to play the final combination, Boi's White queen suddenly morphed into a Black one!

"What do you say to *that*, big Boi," smirked his sultry opponent. "There goes your mate in two."

"On the contrary," said Boi to girl. "I still have a mate in two!"

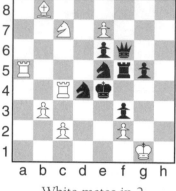

White mates in 2

The lady looked at the board for a moment and disappeared in a huff, not to mention a puff of smoke. Boi thought he might have been playing against the devil.

4.

Twin problems—two (or more) separate but closely related positions—offer tantalizing challenges to composer and solver alike. Sometimes the two positions are identical except that one is shifted up, down, left, or right; often a single piece is relocated. The solutions, of course, though often thematically related, are always different.

A miniature, in problem parlance, contains no more than seven men in total. This clean construction by the Hungarian-American grandmaster is not only a twin and a miniature, it also has something else going for it.

Pal Benko, *Magyar Sakkélet*, 1974, Special Honorable Mention

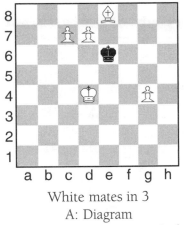

White mates in 3
A: Diagram
B: White king on e3 instead of d4

5.
K. Hannemann, *Skakbladet*, 1922

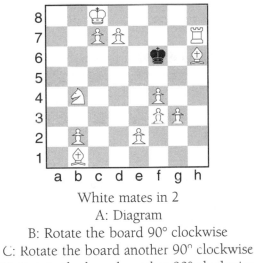

White mates in 2
A: Diagram
B: Rotate the board 90° clockwise
C: Rotate the board another 90° clockwise
D: Rotate the board another 90° clockwise

6.

Pawn promotions are again the keys, but it will take real solving

skill to figure out which men to remove in problems B, C, and D.
I can tell you this: Each problem features a different promotion.

Wolfgang Pauly, *Schachkuriositaten*, 1910

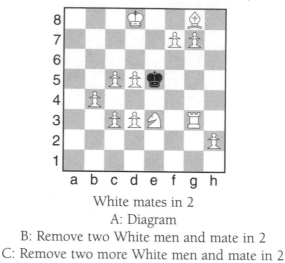

White mates in 2
A: Diagram
B: Remove two White men and mate in 2
C: Remove two more White men and mate in 2
D: Remove two more White men and mate in 2

7.
Tim Krabbé, *Chess Curiosities*, 1985

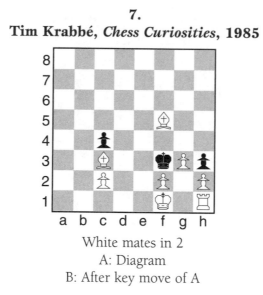

White mates in 2
A: Diagram
B: After key move of A

In this deceptive twin, problem B is contingent on problem A. After solving the diagram position, reset the diagram and play the first move of the solution. This is the setup of problem B.

8.
Assiac (Heinrich Fraenkel),
Adventure in Chess, 1951

White to play. Who is mated?

White plays 1 Bg2+. Is it mate? Evidently not, because Black has the defense 1 ... d5. Is *that* mate? White can now play 2 cxd6 e.p. Mate again!

Checkmate is defined as a condition in which the mated side can neither move the king out of check nor capture or block the mating piece. White argues that since the Black pawn never actually reaches d5 (the en passant capture removes it on the square d6), the move 1 ... d5 does not defend against the check and 1 Bg2+ is actually mate.

You be the judge. What's your opinion?

Constructive Constructions

The positions in this section are properly called puzzles rather than problems, since the latter term has specific meanings and implications that don't apply here. Some of them are constructions meant more for display than for solving. A few others do ask to be solved but not by finding a mate—at least not in the ordinary way.

9.

This position is a record construction task. You should have no trouble figuring out what's going on.

H.H. Cross, *Problemist Fairy Supplement*, 1936

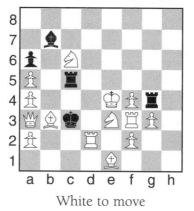

White to move

10.

This record position demonstrates the maximum number of possible checkmates in one move. How many are there?

H. Pöllmacher, R. Schurig, A. Barbe, M. Bezzel, V. Grimm, LaForest, *Illustrierte Zeitung*, 1859

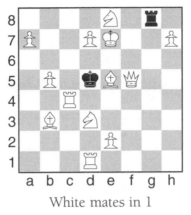

White mates in 1

11.

Jürgen Gelitz, *Die Schwalbe*, 1968

Another record: there are 47 squares on which the Black king would stand legally mated. Disregarding the squares with pieces on them already, that means there are three squares on which the king would *not* be legally mated. Which three?

12.

Construct a position using all eight White pieces (king, queen, both rooks, both bishops, and both knights) in which the pieces have the maximum total moves. The theoretical maximum is 105 moves, with the queen in the center having 27 moves, the rooks 14 each, the bishops 13 each, the knights 8 each, and the king 8. But this cannot be achieved because the pieces get in one another's way. What's the best you can do?

13.

What is the maximum number of men that can be placed on the board in a legal position so that no man guards or attacks any other? Before the meeting of the Problem Commission of the International Chess Federation (FIDE) at Bournemouth in 1989, the number was believed to be 26. But at that meeting John Beasley and 10 other composers found a way to place 27 men. Before looking at their solution, try it yourself to appreciate how difficult it is.

14.
W.A. Shinkman, 1929

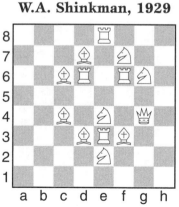

Make a single move with each piece to create a position in which no piece is guarding any other

15.

A few decades ago, when I was executive editor of R.H.M. Press, a now-defunct publisher of chess books, I helped host a meeting of the world's top grandmasters during a very strong international tournament. The purpose of the meeting was to ask the players to contribute chapters to a book to be called *How to Open a Chess Game*.

Some of the grandmasters arrived early. I produced a pocket chess set and passed around the little puzzle below to kill some time while we waited for the others. Several minutes passed while they studied it. Then a few more. I was getting worried. Finally Paul Keres came up with one of the solutions (there's more than one). Can you outsolve the world's greatest chess masters?

Anonymous, 15th century

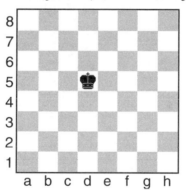

Place four White rooks on the board one at a time, giving check with each of them and checkmate with the fourth. Black moves normally.

16.

If you've ever wanted to try your hand at problem composing, here's your chance.

T.R. Dawson, 1935

Add six Black pieces (including the king) and six Black
pawns so that Black is mated; removing any Black
piece or pawn spoils the mate

17.
Sam Loyd, *Chess Monthly*, 1858

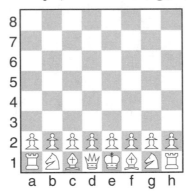

Place the Black king on the board,
then White mates in 3

18.
Karl Fabel, *Die Schwalbe*, 1942

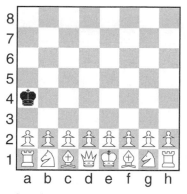

Construct the shortest game to reach this position

19.
Anonymous

White moves first. Black mirrors White's moves exactly, and White mates on the fourth move. What are the moves?

20.

Using only a White king, two White rooks, and a Black king, construct a position in which White can mate Black in four different ways

21.
M. Techritz

Place the two kings and White mates in 1

22.
Eric Angelini, *Europe Echecs*, 1990

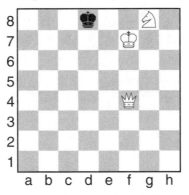

Add one square to the board and White mates in 2

The added square must be adjacent to one of the board edges, of course.

Let's Work It Out Together

In competitive chess, the two players, represented by White and Black, are opponents trying to checkmate each other. In a composed chess problem, the solver plays both sides. White and Black are opponents as usual, but only White tries to give mate while Black tries to avoid it. White, moving first, must give mate in a given number of moves; if he can't, the problem is unsound, or "cooked," as problemists say. On the other hand, if White can mate in more than one way, the problem contains a "dual" and is considered inferior.

In helpmate problems the fundamental rivalry between the two sides is turned on its head. Now the two sides are not opponents but collaborators. As in orthodox problems, the composer sets up the pieces and envisages a position a certain number of moves hence in which Black is mated. The solver's task is to reach that position in the stated number of moves but with the two sides cooperating. Black, who usually moves first in a helpmate, helps White achieve the mating position.

Selfmate problems restore the two sides' rivalry but reverse their roles. This time White, moving first, tries to *force* Black to deliver the mate in a stated number of moves while Black's task is to just say no.

23.
Hermann Albertz and Karl Henke,
Die Schwalbe, 1948

Helpmate in 2; set

Many helpmate problems include "set play," a line of play that would fulfill the conditions of the problem if it were the other player's turn to move. Since Black normally moves first in a help-mate, the set play begins with White: 1 Qxh4 0-0 2 Qh7 mate. But it's Black's move, not White's.

24.

In this and the next problem, don't be concerned that the moves make absolutely no sense in the normal way. These are similar to what problemists call "shortest proof games" (SPGs). The object of an SPG is not to checkmate the opponent but to reach a given configuration in the fewest moves from the opening position. In this problem, a "proof game" (PG), the object is somewhat different, since the final position is not given but is for you to discover.

Pal Benko, Chess Life & Review, 1976
From the starting position, play a game in which
the sixth and final move is both an en passant capture
and a discovered mate. White moves first and the
two sides collaborate.

25.
P. Rösler, *Problemkiste*, 1994

From the starting position, play a game ending with
the move 6 gxf8=N mate.

26.
Noam D. Elkies, Original

A: Reach this position in 4 moves
B: Reach this position in 4.75 moves

27.

This selfmate problem was created some 25 years ago by a member of the Fanatic games club at Twente University in Holland. It was sent to me by Christian Freeling, an inventor of abstract strategy games, notably the great chess variant Grand Chess.

D. Bost, Fanatic Games Club, Twente University, Holland, c. 1972

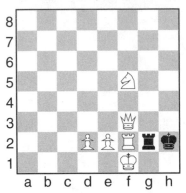

White to play and force Black to give
mate in 29 moves

Despite the 29-move solution, the problem is of only medium difficulty.

28.

You already know what a helpmate is. In a series helpmate, Black, moving first, plays a series of consecutive moves uninterrupted by White, arriving after the specified number of moves (in this case 3) at a position in which White can deliver immediate mate.

Adrian Storisteanu, *Buletin Problemistic,* **1996**

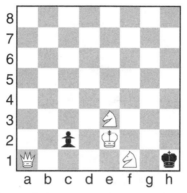

Series helpmate in 3; two solutions

Although dual solutions are usually frowned upon, sometimes the composer includes them intentionally to achieve an effect not otherwise possible. In such cases the problem is like a twin except that the two positions are the same.

29.

Long problem solutions usually make me turn the page fast. Series helpmates, though, are more like puzzles, and you don't have to keep finding the best defense for the other side. Don't be intimidated by the long solution here. Once you realize what the mating move must be and where the Black king has to be at the time, you're on your way.

A. Grigoryan

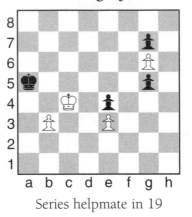

Series helpmate in 19

Black makes 19 moves in a row while White snoozes. After Black's 19th move, White wakes up and delivers checkmate.

30.

Helpnotmate is a rare, not to say unique, stipulation. This was the first one ever published.

Pal Benko, *Chess Life & Review*, 1976

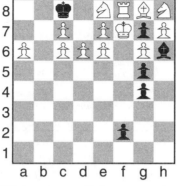

White moves; helpnotmate in 3

When I was the editor of *Chess Life & Review* (now *Chess Life*), I asked Grandmaster Benko to try composing a problem in which the two sides collaborate *not* to checkmate Black in three moves. In a traditional helpmate, White and Black conspire to checkmate; here the goal is just the opposite.

After creating this problem, Benko told me, "There's a couple of ideas in it, but you can't make many of them—it's too limited. And it's not hard to solve—even you can solve it."

Take That Back!

An orthodox chess problem must be *legal* according to the Laws of Chess. It can't have too many men; the pawn structure must be reachable from the opening position by legal moves; the side not on the move must have had a previous legal move; and so on. All of which implies that the position has a history.

A large category of chess composition is based on retrograde analysis; that is, proving by rigorous logic exactly what that history was, if only the last move or two. Retrograde analysis is the subject of the next section; here we are concerned with one of its most fascinating and popular subcategories, the retractor.

In a typical retractor, one or both players take back one or more moves and play different moves that lead to mate in a specified number of "forward" moves; that is, moves played from the position after the retractions.

Composers of retractors are very tricky. One possibility you should always consider is that the retracted move might have been a capture. "Uncaptures" are hard to spot, but I'll let you in on a secret: a pawn on its sixth rank might suggest the possibility of a previous en passant capture.

31.
Julio Sunyer, *Chess Amateur*, 1923

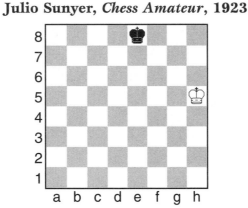

White retracts a move, then Black retracts a move and
plays a different move, then White mates in 1

32.
Bruno Sommer, 1910

White retracts his last move and mates in 1

33.

Hauke Reddmann sent me this elegant miniature along with a comment that it had been inspired by an old T.R. Dawson problem on the same theme. Dawson, whose problem had nine men, claimed it was impossible to show this theme in a miniature, which requires no more than seven men. "I couldn't let that provocation go," Reddmann writes.

Hauke Reddmann, *Die Schwalbe*, 1986

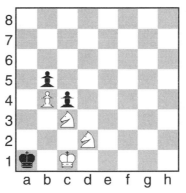

White retracts his last move and then mates in 2

34.
Karl A.K. Larsen, *Arbejder Skak*, 1949

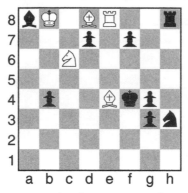

White retracts his last move and mates in 1
A: Diagram
B: Black knight on c3 instead of h3

35.
Vladimir Nabokov was the only great writer who was also an accomplished composer of chess problems. This clever retractor, which he dedicated to the well-known chess master E. Znosko-Borovsky, first appeared under Nabokov's pen name at the time, V. Sirin, in a Russian-language émigré newspaper in Paris.

Vladimir Nabokov, *Poslednie novosti*, Paris, 1932

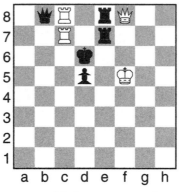

White retracts his last move and mates in 1

36.

Do the rules of tournament play apply to problems? In this one they do.

Jean-Michel Trillon, *Thèmes-64*, 1969

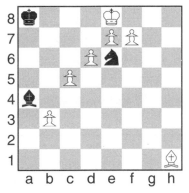

The last player retracts his move: Who wins?
A: Diagram
B: White pawn on e5 instead of c5

37.
R. Kofman, *Shakhmatniy Biulletin*, 1958

White retracts his last move, then mates in 3

This amazing problem in chess logic is difficult to solve but very much worth studying. I'll give you one little hint: If Black castles, White will have no hope of mating him anytime soon.

Remembrance of Things Past

Retrograde analysis is a method of logically determining a position's history to prove or disprove its legality or to establish whether or not castling or en passant is available. The logic must be rigorous; no guesswork is allowed. Composers usually set various traps and red herrings to catch the lazy solver!

But problem composers work within certain agreed conventions. The most important of these in retro problems concern castling and en passant captures. Here's the crucial rule: *Castling is always legal unless proved illegal; en passant captures are always illegal unless proved legal.*

38.

Let's begin with a tutorial.

H. Kamstra, *Tijdschrift NSB*, 1929

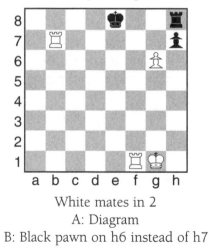

White mates in 2
A: Diagram
B: Black pawn on h6 instead of h7

39.
Sam Loyd, *Musical World*, 1859(?)

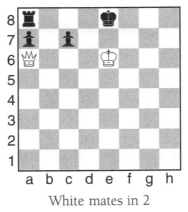

White mates in 2

40.
Dr. Niels Høeg, *Skakbladet*, 1916

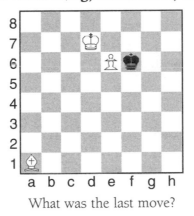

What was the last move?

First, Black is in check, so the last move could not have been by Black. Second, the checking piece, the bishop on a1, could not have made the last move. It could have arrived at a1 only from elsewhere on the same diagonal, which means that Black would have been already in check with White to move. White's king could not have made the last move either.

That leaves the White pawn on e6. Using the same reasoning as before, we know it didn't get there from e5 because Black

41

would have been in check. So how *did* it get there? Careful now.

41.
Raymond Smullyan, 1980

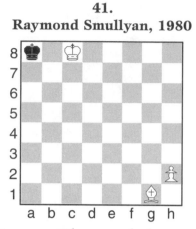

White to move. What were the last two moves?

42.

George Koltanowski has had many careers in chess: competitive player; record-holder in simultaneous blindfold play; lecturer, raconteur, and performer of phenomenal feats of memory; author; distinguished president of the U.S. Chess Federation; and, least known among his many talents, problem composer.

G. Koltanowski,
America Salutes Comins Mansfield, 1983

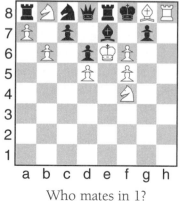

Who mates in 1?

43.
J. Perkins, *Chess*, 1950

White mates in 1

44.
Anonymous, *Skakbladet*, 1924

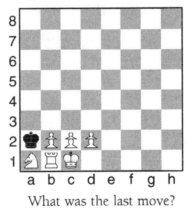

What was the last move?

45.
Karl Fabel,
Braunschweiger Neueste Nachrichten, 1926

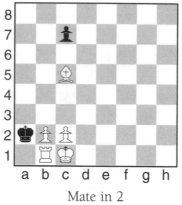

Mate in 2

46.
N.G.G. van Dijk, *Østlendingen*, 1959

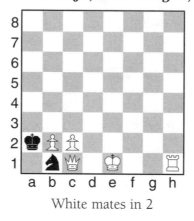

White mates in 2

47.
Werner Keym, *Die Schwalbe*, 1979

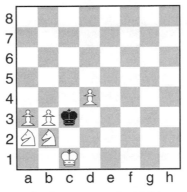

What were the last moves by White and Black?

48.
Karl Fabel, *Deutsche Schachblätter*, 1950

Place the Black king; then White mates in 1

49.
T.R. Dawson, 1927

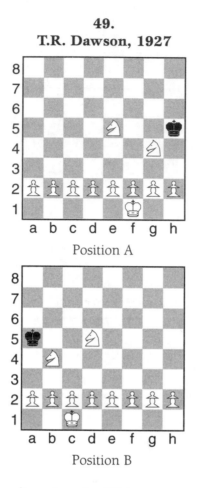

Position A

Position B

In each position, first place the White queen on a legal square, then play a move for White that stalemates Black. Since the positions are mirror images, shouldn't the solutions be mirror images too?

50.
Werner Keym

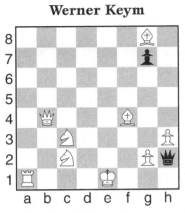

Place the Black king; then mate in 1

51.
Dr. Neils Høeg, *Skakbladet*, 1924

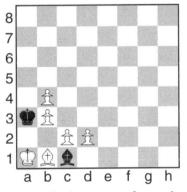

What was the last move for each side?

52.
T.R. Dawson, *Falkirk Herald*, 1914

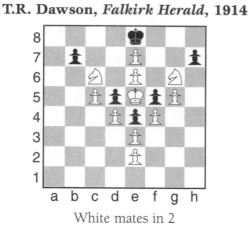

White mates in 2

It's obvious that neither White knight can give mate in the required two moves, and that no White pawn is in position to be promoted. The killing blow will therefore have to be delivered by a pawn. With two Black pawns standing alongside White pawns on the fifth rank, there's definitely a whiff of Calvin Klein's *En Passant* in the air.

53.
Sam Loyd, 1891

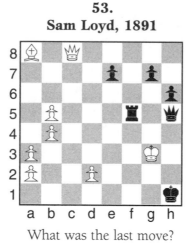

What was the last move?

Since Black is in check, the last move must have been made by White. How did the bishop get to a8? It could not have come

from somewhere on the a8-h1 diagonal because it would already
have been checking the Black king. Could it be a promoted pawn
(after a7-a8=B or b7xa8=B)?

54.
Hand me that retroanalyzer, Doctor!

Adrian Storisteanu, *Rex Multiplex* 1983, 1st prize

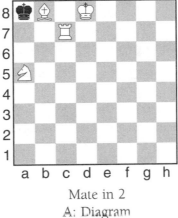

Mate in 2
A: Diagram
B: Rotate board 90° clockwise

55.
Composer unknown, *Chess Life & Review*, 1976

White has been mated. What was the last move?

56.

This problem was created to make a point about retroanalyzing the right to castle.

Armand Lapierre, *Thèmes 64*, 1959,
4th Honorable Mention

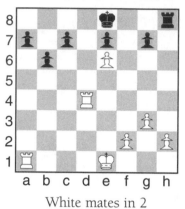

White mates in 2

57.

L. Ceriani, *Sahovski Vjesnik* 1951, 1st prize

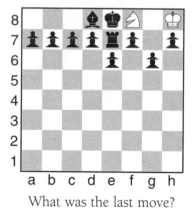

What was the last move?

58.

Remember this old conundrum? One side of a card says THE STATEMENT ON THE OTHER SIDE IS FALSE. The other side says THE STATEMENT ON THE OTHER SIDE IS TRUE. To close this section, here's a similarly perverse puzzle that should have retro lawyers climbing the walls.

W. Langstaff, *Chess Amateur*, 1922

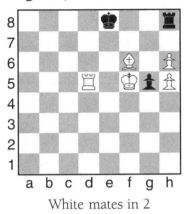

White mates in 2

Various Variants

Chess players think of other chesslike games as variants of chess. But the fact is that chess itself is a variant of an ancient game that hundreds of years ago developed in several different directions. Sister games include shogi, Korean chess, and Chinese chess (xiangqi), each of which is played by many millions of people in various parts of the world.

Chess itself has been the basis for innumerable variants. David Pritchard's great study, *The Encyclopedia of Chess Variants*, describes about 1,450 variants, and new ones come out every year. Some variants are better suited to problem composition than to competitive play. A few of the most interesting or amusing of these are found in this section.

59.

In an orthodox "direct mate" problem, White moves first and Black tries to avoid being mated in the specified number of moves. In a helpmate, as we saw earlier, Black moves first and, instead of avoiding mate, tries to help White deliver the final blow in the specified number of moves. Think of it as a puzzle in which you use the pieces of both sides and normal chess rules to set up a mate position.

In the position below, an extra rule has been added: It is illegal to give check unless it's checkmate.

T. Steudel, B. Rehm, A.H. Kniest,
Diagramen u. Figuren, **1963**

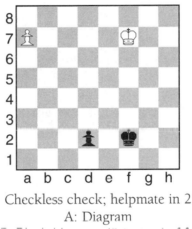

Checkless check; helpmate in 2
A: Diagram
B: Black king on d5 instead of f2

60.

Now that you know how checkless chess operates, try this nice problem by the greatest pioneer of unorthodox chess problems.

T.R. Dawson, *Die Welt*, 1951

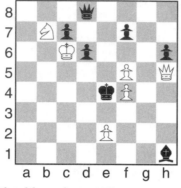

Checkless chess; White mates in 2

61.

Ronald Turnbull, *diagrammes*, 1994

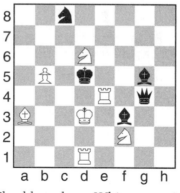

Checkless chess; White mates in 2

1 Kc2+, for instance, is illegal because of 1 ... Bd2 (not 1 ... Bxd1+, which is illegal because it's check but not mate). And 1 Kc3+ is illegal because Black has 1 ... Bxd1 (not 1 ... Bd2+ because it's check but not mate). So you'll have to find something else.

62.
H.P. Rehm, 1971

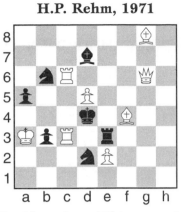

Checkless chess; White mates in 2

63.

This problem demonstrates Circe, an entertaining variant invented by Pierre Monréal in 1967 that has become a popular problem theme. The variant was named for the Greek sorceress who turned Ulysses' companions into swine.

A. Goset and J. Oudot, *Problème*, 1969

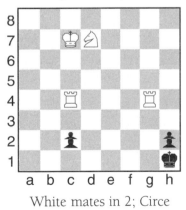

White mates in 2; Circe

The rules are simple. A captured man is immediately put back on its square of origin, but if that square is occupied, the man is removed from play like a captured man in orthodox chess. A rook, knight, or bishop is returned to the starting square of the color it's captured on (that is, a rook captured on d5 is returned to h1; if h1 is occupied, the rook is lost); a captured pawn goes to the second/seventh rank on the capturing file. A reborn pawn regains its double-space first move, and a reborn rook is eligible for castling. Kings are not captured. Important: A capture is illegal if replacing the captured man checks the capturing player.

64.
Zdenek Libis and Mark Ridley, *The Problemist*, 1989

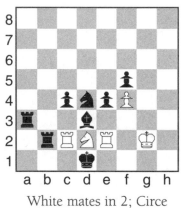

White mates in 2; Circe

If it were Black's move and he captured either White rook with his king, the rook would be replaced on h1 (because it's a white square). It would then be White's move, and he would play either Re1 mate or Rc1 mate (depending on whether Black had taken the rook on e2 or c2). Absurd as it looks, the rook on e1 (or c1) would be immune from capture because it would be replaced on a1 *with check*, which is against the Circe rules! This is also why, in the diagram, Black can't take either rook with his rook, knight, or bishop.

65.
Adrian Storisteanu, *Europe Echecs*, 1976

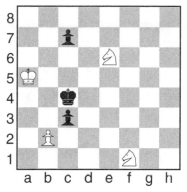

Black to move; helpmate in 3; Circe

66.
Adrian Storisteanu, *Phènix*, 1990

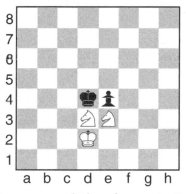

White to move; helpstalemate in 3; Circe

Whoa! Helpstalemate? *And* Circe?

Don't be scared. The objective is simply this: White moves first and the two sides collaborate to produce a position after three moves in which Black is stalemated. Circe adds a little complication, but you should be able to handle it by now.

In helpmates (and helpstalemates), Black traditionally moves first. The composer says the White-to-move stipulation here is "quite unfortunate," but notes that only five pieces were needed.

67.

The rule in optional replacement chess, explains the composer of this problem, is that "a player making a capture may if he wishes replace the captured man on any vacant square (a bishop on a square of the same color, a pawn not on the first or eighth rank)."

John Beasley, *British Chess Magazine,* **1992**

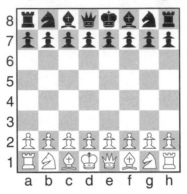

Optional replacement chess, position after Black's 4th move; what were the moves?

Starting from the standard opening position, play four moves for both sides to reach the diagram position. Notice that the positions of the White king and queen are reversed.

68.

In cylinder chess, you are to imagine that the a-file and h-file are contiguous; that is, joined as if the board were wrapped around a vertical cylinder. This variant, of unknown origin, first appeared as a game about two hundred years ago and was introduced as a problem theme by the composer of this work in 1907.

A. Piccinini, *Revista Scacchistica Italiana*, 1907

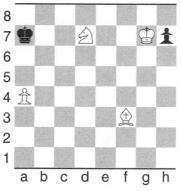

Cylinder chess; White mates in 2

69.

According to David Pritchard, in *The Encyclopedia of Chess Variants*, a move around the cylinder that leaves the position unchanged is disallowed, but problemists disagree. The 1958 Piran Codex, in which problemists agreed to observe certain conventions in problem composition, specifically allows a move to encircle the cylinder and end up on its starting square.

W.A. Mongredien, *Bulletin de la FFE*, #19, 1926

Cylinder chess; White mates in 2

70.

Here's a little foretaste of what to expect later in this book. It's a cylinder chess problem, so it belongs here, but it's not entirely kosher.

John Beasley,
Blue Danube Joke Tourney, 1993, 3d prize

Cylinder chess; should White resign?

71

Losing chess is one of the most vibrant forms of unorthodox chess, offering fertile ground both for players and problem composers. Its precise origins are unknown, but it is probably 150 years old, if not older. Though the rules have never been standardized, the most widely accepted, according to David Pritchard in *The Encyclopedia of Chess Variants*, are these:

1. Capturing is compulsory. If more than one capture is possible, the capturing player chooses which to make.

2. There is no check and the king is not royal, which means it can be captured like any other piece and can move next to the enemy king (and be captured by it).

3. A pawn can promote to a king as well as any other piece of its color (but not a pawn).

4. The object is to lose all one's men or be left without a move (stalemate). The first player to achieve this goal wins the game.

Here's a fairly simple demonstration.

T.R. Dawson, *Deutsches Wochenschach*, 1925

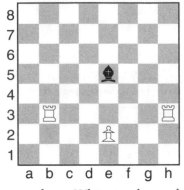

Losing chess; White to play and win

72.
John Beasley, Original

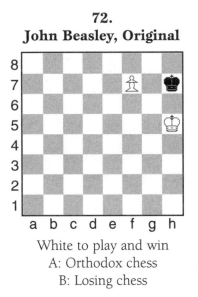

White to play and win
A: Orthodox chess
B: Losing chess

73.

In this intriguing and as yet unexplored variant by T.R. Dawson, any man that is guarded by another man of the same color may not move. A pinned piece does not function as a guard because it cannot legally move.

T.R. Dawson, *Caissa's Fairy Tales*, 1947

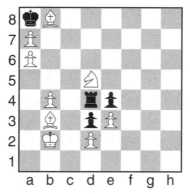

White mates in 2; guarded men may not move

74.

Don't you sometimes wish you could make two moves in a row? In double-move chess you can! Double-move chess is a variant of Marseillais chess, which was popularized in the 1920s by the Marseilles native Albert Fortis and attracted such luminaries as Alekhine and Reti. The Marseillais rules are largely ignored in this variant. The only rules that matter here are: 1. Each player makes two consecutive moves each turn with the same piece or different pieces. 2. There is no check. 3. The object is to capture the opposing king.

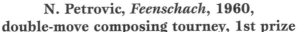

N. Petrovic, *Feenschach*, 1960,
double-move composing tourney, 1st prize

Double-move chess; White mates in 3 double moves

75.

Here's another wish granted: the right to refuse an opponent's move! In refusal chess, invented in 1958 by Fred Galvin, a player may refuse an opponent's move but must then accept the alternative. The only exception is that a king must always get out of check. In this problem, however, contrary to the usual rules, a king that has only one move to get out of check loses if that move is refused by the opponent!

C.H.O'D. Alexander, *The Problemist*, **March 1970**

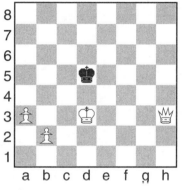

Refusal chess; White mates in 2

76.

In grid chess the board is divided into a grid of 16 2x2 sections. A man may move only to a different grid section (just as in orthodox chess a man moves to a different square). The strange consequence of this rule is that two pieces in the same grid section have no effect on each other. In the position below, for example, the Black king is not in check although it's on intimate terms with an enemy rook. Moving the White rook to g2, say, would check the king, but that's not the correct solution, of course.

G.H. Drese, *Le Minotaure,* **1971**

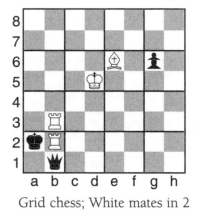

Grid chess; White mates in 2

77.

Thomas Rayner Dawson, the most prolific problem experimenter and composer, invented scores of new pieces, board configurations, tasks, and unusual stipulations. One of them is the "watchtower" theme used here. A specific piece, designated a "watchtower," functions normally (e.g., it can give check) but does not move.

T.R. Dawson, Reading *Observer*, August 12, 1912

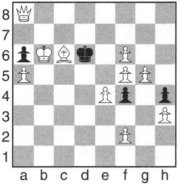

White mates in 8 with the queen,
which does not move

78.

In billiards chess, pieces carom off the sides of the board like billiard balls. In this variant's early form, of which this position is an example, only bishops and queens had that power—and it's a great power indeed, as you will see. The carom, by the way, must describe a right angle. For instance, a bishop moving from e2 to h5 caroms off the edge of the board along the h5-e8 diagonal, then continuing, if desired, along the e8-a4 diagonal, and so on.

F.F.L. Alexander and E.P. White,
The Problemist, **June 1932**

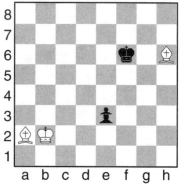

Billiards chess; White mates in 2

79.

The imitator is a strange, fascinating beast. It moves parallel to and simultaneously with whatever piece of either color is being moved. If the imitator can't do so without falling off the board or bumping into another man, then the move it's trying to imitate is not legal.

John Beasley after J.E.H. Creed, *The Problemist*, 1989

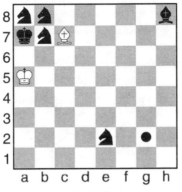

Imitator on g2; White mates in 2

For example, White can move 1 Kb6, and the imitator goes to h3. The White king is not in check because Black can't play 1 ... Kxb6 or Nxb6, which would force the imitator southeast off the board. But the Black king *is* in check, since White threatens 2 Kxa7 (Ig4). Black has only one defense: 1 ... Bf6 (If1). By pushing the imitator behind the knight on e2 and preventing it from moving along the f1-a6 diagonal, the bishop move stops 2 Kxa7.

80.

A neutral pawn belongs to both sides and can be moved or captured by either. It remains neutral after promotion, so if White tries to give mate by 1 c8=nQ+, Black, regarding the new queen as his own, says "thank you very much indeed!" and plays 1 ... QxK. Notice! A neutral piece can check either king, so 1 c8=nQ+ is illegal because of self-check!

Kurt Smulders, *HM Europe Echecs,* **1970 (version)**

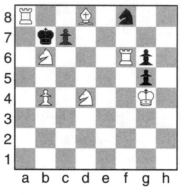

Neutral pawn on c7; White mates in 2

81.

Berkeleian Chess is one of the more bizarre problem themes. It works like this: Any piece, including a king, that is neither attacked by an enemy man nor guarded by a friendly man is removed from the board.

The idea is a joking reference to the 18th-century philosopher George Berkeley, who proposed that material things exist only because they are perceived to exist.

L.C. Rodó, *El Acertijo*, 1993

Berkeleian Chess; find the move that makes all the pieces disappear

Every man on both sides is, for the moment, either attacked or guarded. By making the correct first move (you'll have to figure out whether it's a White move or a Black one), you will set in motion a chain of disappearing pieces resulting in a completely empty board. You need to make only a single move and then remove the affected pieces one by one. What is that move?

82.

It may not be true that inventors of chess variants and composers of unorthodox chess problems have warped minds, though it's an understandable assumption. What they certainly do have is a sense of humor.

Fuddled men, a droll conception by John Beasley, the long-time problem editor for the *British Chess Magazine* and an eminent constructor, have had too much to drink and must stop and think after each move. This means that a fuddled man can't make two moves in succession. An immobilized piece makes no threat, of course. You take it from there.

John Beasley, *British Chess Magazine*, 1987

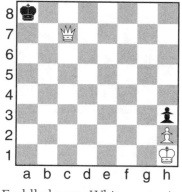

Fuddled men; White mates in 2

83.

Here are the essential (somewhat oversimplified) rules of kriegspiel, a chess variant invented by Henry Michael Temple and introduced in 1898: The two sides play on separate boards and can see only their own pieces. They cannot see and are not told the opponent's moves. Between the players is an umpire with a concealed third board on which the actual positions of both sides' pieces are represented.

The umpire tells each player when it's his turn to move, reports a capture by naming the square on which it took place (but not the pieces involved), disallows illegal moves, and announces check. Otherwise he is silent except to answer one specific question. A player may ask "Are there any?" (often abbreviated to "Any?"), meaning "Are there any pawn captures?" If a pawn capture is possible, the umpire must say "Yes," in which case the player must attempt a pawn capture. If not, the umpire says "No," and the player may try some other move. Pawn tries are an essential component of kriegspiel strategy.

But not in this remarkable problem, which demonstrates another element of kriegspiel logic.

John Beasley, Original

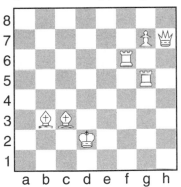

Kriegspiel. White has captured everything but the
Black king. Can White now mate in 1?

Trick or Treat

I've noted earlier that problemists are bound by certain conventions designed to ensure that a composition is legal and fair so that the solver knows the solution can be found by dint of honest intellectual labor.

I've also mentioned that problemists have a sense of humor. Some of them have contributed compositions to a class of problems that are illegal and/or unfair and deliberately flout convention. There's nothing wrong with that, of course, as long as the solver understands that in such cases orthodox analytic methods will not yield a solution. If problem composers have perverse imaginations, so should solvers.

You have been warned.

84.
H. Fischer, 1910

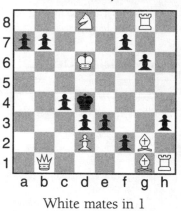

White mates in 1

If you have trouble solving this puzzle by studying the diagram, set up the position on an actual board and the solution will reveal itself.

85.
Dr. H. Burgmann, *Die Welt*, 1952

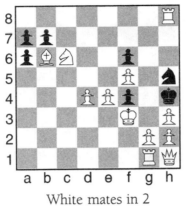

White mates in 2

Is there really a mate in two? Nothing seems to work. What's going on here?

86.
Noam D. Elkies, version of an anonymous puzzle

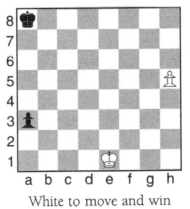

White to move and win

When it comes to outrageous chess problems, this one ranks pretty high. Noam Elkies sent it to me with the warning that it's "an old joke."

87.
T.R. Dawson, Reading *Observer*, 1913

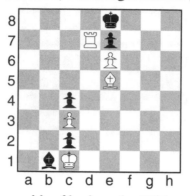

Black gave odds of both rooks; White mates in 4

88.
Anonymous, *British Chess Magazine*, 1993

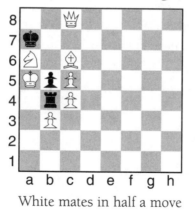

White mates in half a move

89.

In this problem, and a few others in this section, "long castling" takes on a whole new meaning.

John Beasley, *British Chess Magazine,* **1993**
Version of Seret, 1971

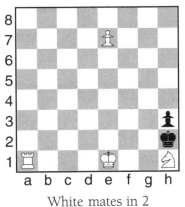

White mates in 2

90.

Tim Krabbé, *Schaakbulletin,* **1972**

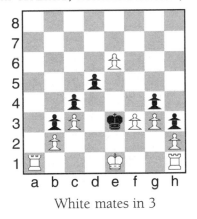

White mates in 3

Whenever you see a position with the king and at least one rook on their original squares you have to consider the possibility that castling is involved (though sometimes it's a red herring). Let's see part of the solution: 1 e7 gxf3 2 e8=Q+ Kd3 3 0-0-0 mate. Or if 1 ... Kd3 2 e8=Q Kc2 3 Qe2 mate. If 1 ... d4 2 e8=Q+ and 3 Qe2 mate. If Black tries 1 ... Kxf3, he's mated with 2 e8=R! (2 e8=Q? Kg2! and there's no mate) 2 ... d4 3 0-0 mate.

But after 1 e7 Kxf3 2 e8=R Kg2, what happens now?

91.
Noam D. Elkies, Internet, 1991

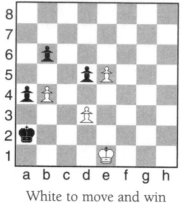

White to move and win

92.

When I published this in my "just for fun" column in Chess Life & Review, I called it an "infuriating illegitimacy." I'm sure you'll agree.

James Stevenson, *Chess Life & Review*, 1976

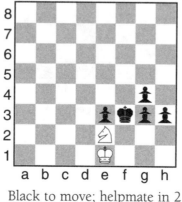

Black to move; helpmate in 2

93.

Just when you think you've seen everything ...

Bedrich Formanek, *Pravda* (Czechoslovakia), 1984

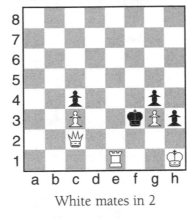

White mates in 2

94.

F.W. von Holzhausen, *Die Welt*, 1961

Place any piece on any empty square; then White
moves and stalemates Black

When you see the solution you'll probably want to murder von
Holzhausen for creating this problem, and me for including it in
this book. Read the stipulation carefully, take a deep breath, and
count to 10.

95.

Even though problemists sometimes deliberately break the rules to make a point or just for fun, the imaginary players in their imaginary games don't always have that luxury.

José Paluzie, 1910(?)

White moves and mates in 1

96.
Tolosa

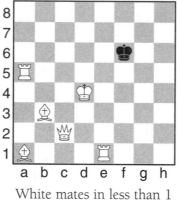

White mates in less than 1

With all those pieces arrayed against the lone king, surely there's a mate. Isn't there?

97.
M. Charosh, *Fairy Chess Review*, 1937

White mates in 0 moves

Huh?

98.
Had enough castling jokes? That's good.

K. Soltsien, *Fairy Chess Review*, 1957

White mates in 1

Promotional Considerations

Whoever in the deep dark recesses of history decided that a pawn could aspire to be more than a pawn gave chess its unique connection with humanity. The ever-forward mobility of the pawn in its striving for a new life is what I think Philidor meant when he said "The pawn is the soul of chess."

The problems in this section, like those in the previous one, are outlaws, but here they all have something to do with promotion. The pawns you will encounter here, not content with ordinary promotion according to the law, indulge in all manner of underpromotion and overpromotion, not to mention outright treason.

99.
J.H. Zukertort

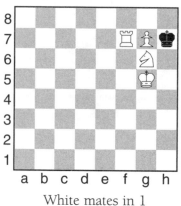

White mates in 1

Yes, this is *the* Zukertort, the 19th-century master who won the great London tournament in 1883 ahead of Steinitz but lost a match to him three years later, after which Steinitz declared himself the first official world champion.

100.
Bedrich Formanek,
Association Slovaque, 1966, 1st prize

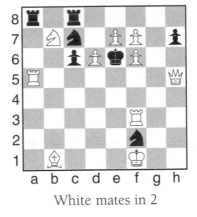

White mates in 2

Try as you might, you will not find a mate in two, not even by promoting to another White piece.

101.
Noam D. Elkics, Original

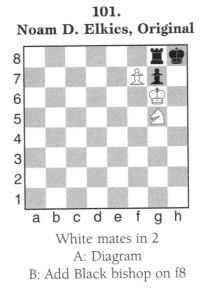

White mates in 2
A: Diagram
B: Add Black bishop on f8

102.

Not quite a century ago, Gyula (Julius) Breyer (1893–1921) was one of the young chess revolutionaries responsible for radical new theories of the opening. His unusually promising playing career was cut tragically short when he died of heart disease at the age of 28. Though not known as a problemist, he composed at least one fine retractor problem and committed this evil but clever felony.

Gyula Breyer, *Magyar Sakkvilag,* **1918**

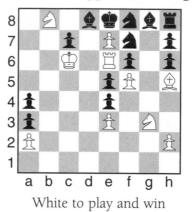

White to play and win

White's rook is attacked, and he must do something decisive right now. Promoting his e-pawn with a capture on d8 or f8 leads nowhere—that is, promoting it to a *White* piece. So think about promoting it to a *Black* piece.

103.
Matt Bengtson, Original

White to move and draw

Any legal move by White loses; for instance, 1 g8=Q Ba3! 2 Qxf7+ Kd8! (2 ... Kxf7? stalemate) and the Black c-pawn will win the game. But what about *illegal* moves?

104.
Emil Palkoska, *The Leader*, 1910

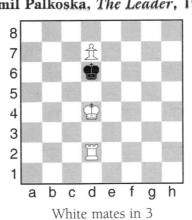

White mates in 3

This is the earliest example I've found of this particular type of underpromotion—or "overpromotion."

105.
Leonid Kubbel, 1941

White mates in 2

It's a puzzlement how to release the stalemate without spoiling the mate at the same time.

106.
John Beasley, version by Noam D. Elkies

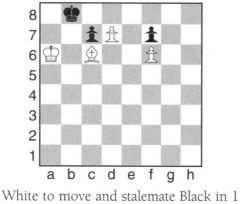

White to move and stalemate Black in 1
A: Diagram
B: Add Black rook on c8

107.

In this book we have seen all sorts of promotions—to major pieces, minor pieces, and even pieces of the wrong color. The type of promotion here—which is none of the above—is not new. Composer John Beasley points out that the idea was used by T.R. Dawson in 1913. Dawson's study, a rather artificial setting, was to force stalemate (see the next problem). Beasley's accomplishment is to force a win.

John Beasley, EBUR, 1996

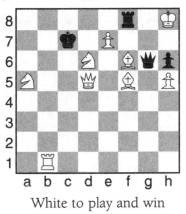

White to play and win

108.

Now that you have met the dummy pawn, say hello to his whole family.

T.R. Dawson, Reading *Observer*, 1913

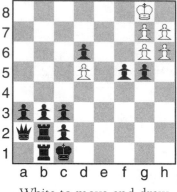

White to move and draw

109.
Juraj Lörinc, 1993

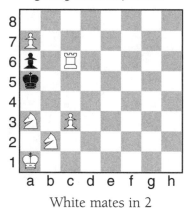

White mates in 2

This promotional frivolity is unlike any of the others. The only thing you can be sure of is that it isn't orthodox.

110.

The last problem in this chapter is easily the most outrageous. The trick it's based on is good to know and can come in quite handy in the right circumstances.

John Beasley and Noam D. Elkies, Original

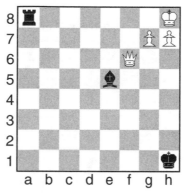

What is White's only hope of avoiding defeat?

You're supposed to imagine that this is the final part of a game between amateurs using a very old chess set in a very old chess club.

The World's Hardest
Chess Problem

111.
Composer and date unknown

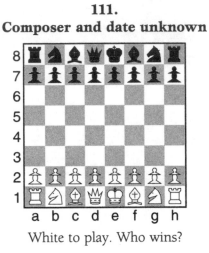

White to play. Who wins?

Solutions

1. 1 Rc6+ is the only move that is not mate. Black shouldn't worry that by capturing the checking bishop on h7 he is exposing his king to checkmate by the other bishop on a8. White's rook, which allows the check from h7, at the same time blocks the check from a8.

2. Put the pawn on h2. White then mates with 1 h4 gxh4 e.p. 2 Bxg6 mate.

3. White queen: 1 Nxe6 (threat: Rxd4 mate) 1 ... Nc6 2 Qxf5 mate, or 1 ... Rxf6 2 Rxe5 mate, or 1 ... Nxc4 2 Qxd4 mate. Not 1 Nb5 because of 1 ... Rxf6, freeing the f5 square.

Black queen: 1 Nb5, threatening Rxd4 mate. If 1 ... Nxc4 or Nc6 or Kd5 then 2 Nc3 mate.

4. A: 1 d8=B Kd6 2 c8=R Ke6 3 Rc6 mate.
B: 1 d8=Q Ke5 2 c8=N Ke6 3 Qd6 mate.
Each of the four promotions is to a different piece.

5. A remarkable achievement. The key move in each of the four positions is a pawn promotion, and the four promotions are in descending order: queen, rook, bishop, knight.
A: 1 d8=Q+ Ke6 2 Qe7 mate.
B: 1 b8=R Kf4 2 Rf8 mate.
C: 1 d8=B Kd4 2 Bf6 mate.
D: 1 f8=N Kd5 2 Bb7 mate.

6. Each solution involves a different pawn promotion but on the same square:
A: 1 f8=N Kf4 2 Ng6 mate; or 1 ... Kf6 2 Nd7 mate.
B: Remove the pawns on c5 and h2: 1 f8=R Kd6 2 Nc4 mate.
C: Remove the pawns on d5 and g7: 1 f8=B Kf6 2 Bg7 mate; or 1 ... Kf4 2 Bd6 mate.
D: Remove the pawn on d3 and the bishop on g8: 1 f8=Q Ke6 2 Qe7 mate; or 1 ... Ke4 2 Qf5 mate.

7. A: 1 Ke1 Kg2 2 Be4 mate.
B: In this position, White's king is on e1, having moved there to start the solution of problem A. 1 0-0 Ke2 2 Bg4 mate. The double solution starting with A: 1 Kg1 Ke2 2 Bg4 mate doesn't work because with the king on g1 there is no solution for B, as there is with the king on e1. Since each

twin is a separate problem, castling in position B can't be disproved and is therefore legal. As I will have occasion to point out again, castling in problems is always legal unless it can be proved illegal by retrograde analysis (i.e., by showing that the king or rook has already moved).

8. The position on the board takes precedence over all other considerations. White's 1 Bg2+ is not mate. Since Black can play 1 … d5+, all the conditions of a White checkmate are not present. After 1 … d5 the position on the board *does* meet all the conditions for checkmate, but this time in Black's favor. White has no legal move that changes the naked fact of mate, and the game is over.

9. Every move by White is checkmate—29 in all, the highest number thus far achieved without promoted men. But what is the maximum number of checkmates possible if the position includes nonmating moves? To find out, see the following position by Pöllmacher et al.

10. There are 47 mates, the current record: a8=Q, a8=B, Rc8, Rc7, Rc6, Rc5, Rc3, Rc2, Rcc1, Ra4, Rb4, Rd4, Re4, Rf4, Rg4, Rh4, Nc1, Nb2, Nb4, Nc5, Nf4, Nf2, Ne1, d8=Q, d8=R, Nc7, Nf6, Bb8, Bc7, Bd6, Bd4, Bc3, Bb2, Ba1, Bf6, Bg7, Bh8, Bf4, Bg3, Bh2, e4, Qe6, Qf7, Qe4, Qf3, hxg8=Q, hxg8=B.

11. Not b4, b7, or e2, in each case because of an impossible double check.

12. The maximum, as proved mathematically by E. Landau in *Der Schachfreund* in 1899, is 100 moves. Here's how it was done half a century before the mathematicians went to work:

M. Bezzel, *Deutsche Schachzeitung*, 1849

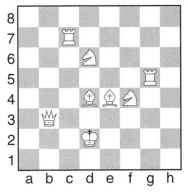

13. This is how they did it:

John Beasley et al., Bournemouth, 1989.
Dedicated to T.R. Dawson by the "Bournemouth Solvers."

This is a legal position. The two extra White knights are promoted pieces, accounted for by the two missing White pawns.

14. Here is one of several sequences: 1 Nf8, 2 Nh8, 3 Bg8, 4 Ng5, 5 Qa4, 6 Bh5, 7 Ng1, 8 Bf1, 9 Bh1, 10 Rd2, 11 Rb6, 12 Rc3, 13 Re7, 14 Bf5.

15. Put the first rook on d2, check. After 1 ... Ke4, for example, put the second rook on g4, check. If now 2 ... Ke5, put the third rook on, say, e2, check, and the fourth rook gives mate on the f-file. The key idea is to put the second rook so as to trap the king on the two files between the rooks.

16.

17. Put the Black king on h4. White then mates with 1 d4 Kg4 2 e4+ Kh4 3 g3 mate; or 1 ... Kh5 2 Qd3 Kg4 (or Kh4) 3 Qh3 mate.

18. 1 Na3 (or Nc3) b5 2 Nxb5 Nf6 3 Nxa7 Ne4 4 Nxc8 Nc3 5 Nxe7 c6 6 Nxc6 Nb1 7 Nxb8 Ra3 8 Nxd7 g5 9 Nxf8 Qd6 10 Nxh7 Kd7 11 Nxg5 Rh4 (or Rc8) 12 Nxf7 Rc4 13 Nxd6 Kc6 14 Nxc4 Kb5 15 Nxa3+ Ka4 16 Nxb1.

19. One solution is 1 d4 d5 2 Qd3 Qd6 3 Qh3 Qh6 4 Qxc8 mate. Another is 1 c4 c5 2 Qa4 Qa5 3 Qc6 Qc3 4 Qxc8 mate.

20.

Karl Fabel, *Die Schwalbe*, 1937

```
8 . . . . . . . .
7 . . . . . . . .
6 . . . . . . . .
5 . . . . . . . .
4 . . . . . . . .
3 . . . . . . . .
2 . . . ♖ . . . .
1 ♚ . . . ♔ . . ♖
  a b c d e f g h
```

The four mates are Kd2, Ke2, Kf2, and 0-0.

21. Put the White king on f3 and the Black king on h1. White plays 1 Kxf2 mate.

22. Add the square e9 and play 1 Ne9 Kxe9 (forced) 2 Qc7 mate.

23. 1 Rh7 0-0 (1 … Rf1? 2 Re7+) 2 Re7 Qc8 mate.

24. 1 e4 e5 2 Qh5 Nc6 3 g4 d6 4 g5 Kd7 5 Bh3+ f5 6 gxf6 e.p. discovered mate!

25. 1 h4 d5 2 h5 Nd7 3 h6 Ndf6 4 hxg7 Kd7 5 Rh6 Ne8 6 gxf8=N mate!

26. A: 1 e4 g5 2 Qh5 Bg7 3 Qxh7 Kf8 4 Qxg8+ Kxg8.
    B: 1 e3 h5 2 Qxh5 Nh6 3 Qxh6 g5 4 Qg7 Bxg7 5 e4 0-.
    That last move is not a typo, but the first half of castling. If Black were to complete the final move, the total number of moves would be 5. But counting White's e4 as the 4.5th move, then half of Black's next move makes the total 4.75. Note that in this problem and in number 25, the move sequences are precisely determined, unlike number 24, where some moves may be transposed.

94

27. 1 Qg3+ Kh1 2 Qh3+ Rh2 3 Qf3+ Rg2 4 d4 Kh2 5 Qg3+ Kh1 6 Qh3+ Rh2 7 Qf3+ Rg2 8 d5 Kh2 9 Qg3+ Kh1 10 Qh3+ Rh2 11 Qf3+ Rg2 12 d6 Kh2 13 Qg3+ Kh1 14 Qh3+ Rh2 15 Qf3+ Rg2 16 d7 Kh2 17 Qg3+ Kh1 18 Qh3+ Rh2 19 Qf3+ Rg2 20 d8=R! Kh2 21 Qg3+ Kh1 22 Qh3+ Rh2 23 Qf3+ Rg2 24 Rg8 Kh2 25 Qg3+ Kh1 26 Qh3+ Rh2 27 Rg2 Rxh3 28 Ng3+ Rxg3 29 Rg1+ Rxg1 mate.

28. 1 c1=B, 2 Bxe3, 3 Bg1, and now White plays Qa8 mate.

1 c1=R, 2 Rxf1, 3 Rg1, and now White plays Qh8 mate.

In each case, the Knight not needed for the mate is removed from the board, and the two mating moves are on the two most distant corners.

29. Since White doesn't move except to deliver the final blow and the executioner can be only a pawn, you have to figure the king will die on a5, done in by the b-pawn: 1 g4, 2 g3, 3 g2, 4 g1=R, 5 Rxg6, 6 Ra6, 7 g5, 8 g4, 9 g3, 10 g2, 11 g1=B, 12 Bxe3, 13 Bb6, 14 e3, 15 e2, 16 e1=N, 17 Nd3, 18 Nc5, 19 Na4, and now White mates with b4. The under-promotions to rook, bishop, and knight are not only pretty but also necessary. Try promoting to queens and see what happens.

30. 1 a7 (anything else is mate) 1 … f1=B! (if 1 … f1=Q+ or R+, the only reply would be 2 Nf6 mate; or if 1 … f1=N White must play 2 a8=N or B, with unavoidable mate on the next move) 2 a8=B! (if 2 a8=N there would be no way to avoid 3 Nb6 mate, among other mates) 2 … Ba6 3 Bb7+ and because Black can play 3 … Bxb7, mate in three has been avoided.

31. White retracts Kg6xRh5, and Black retracts Rh8xQh5. This was the position before those moves:

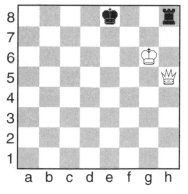

Black plays 0-0, and White mates with Qh7.

32. White's last move was exf6 e.p. Instead, he could have mated Black with 1 e8=Q mate.

33. Since White retracts, the last move must have been his; therefore it is Black's move in the diagram. Unfortunately, however, Black is stalemated and can't move. If he could play 1 ... cxb3 e.p., White could mate him with 2 Nxb3.

White obviously had several possible prior moves here. If he could prove that his last move was b2-b4, Black would be forced to play his only move, cxb3 e.p., and would be summarily mated. To demonstrate that b2-b4 was his last move, White retracts it! And now, to mate in two, White plays the same 1 b2-b4! Black now must play 1 ... cxb3 e.p. and is mated by 2 Nxb3.

Here's the inspiring Dawson problem:

T.R. Dawson, *Chess Review*, 1920

White retracts his last move and then mates in 2

The solution? You already know it! Also see number 2.

34. A: White retracts Ne7xRc6 and plays 1 Nd5 mate. The White piece on c6 has to be a rook or Nd5 is not mate.

B: White retracts Re5xNe8 and plays 1 Bg5 mate. The piece on e8 must be a knight because a rook or queen would pin the bishop on d8, and a bishop cannot be legally situated on e8 because of the pawns on d7 and f7.

35. White retracts the move dxNc8=R and plays instead 1 dxRe8=N mate. The Black piece on c8 must be a knight or White would either be in check or could not mate on e8. "There is some mild magic," Nabokov writes, "in the retrospective transformation of White R into Black Kt, and Black R into White Kt, with the symmetry of pieces (and White's defense of c7) retained."

36. Both kings are in check, and it is clear that the last move could not have been by Black.

A: White retracts his only possible previous move, e5xd6 e.p., which was played after Black advanced his d-pawn to block the check by White's bishop. But that also exposed White's king to check by Black's bishop on a4. Since White's e5xd6 e.p. is illegal because it leaves his king in check, he retracts it, putting his pawn back on e5 and the Black pawn back on d5. The Laws of Chess provide no penalty for touching and not moving a piece that has no legal move—in this case the pawn on e5—so White simply plays 1 bxa4 and wins thanks to his huge material advantage (two pawns are about to promote).

B: With the pawn on e5 instead of c5, the situation is different. Now the illegal move must have been c5xd6 e.p. After restoring the Black pawn to d5 and the White pawn to c5, White is required to move the touched c-pawn to c6, and Black plays Bxc6 mate.

37. White retracts 0-0-0, thereby proving that he had the right to castle (otherwise he wouldn't be able to retract it). But the fact that White can castle means that his king never left e1. If that's the case, how did his king rook get out? Easy: it didn't! The rook must have been captured on h1 (or on h2, g1, or f1). But how then can the rook on d3 be explained? The only explanation is that it's a promoted pawn! White has seven pawns on the board, so the rook on d3 is, or was, the eighth pawn.

Where could it have been promoted? If it were promoted somewhere on the queenside, the Black king at some point could not have been on e8, else the new rook could not have escaped. If the promotion were on e8 or f8, then again the Black king could not have been on e8. If the promotion were on h8, then the Black rook had to have moved at some point. In all these cases, a move by Black's king or rook would mean that Black has lost the right to castle.

That leaves g8. A promotion there might have occurred without infringing Black's right to castle, since a piece on f8 could have shielded the king temporarily and the new rook could have escaped via the g-file.

Only two pawns could have reached g8: the b-pawn or the e-pawn (the a-pawn couldn't get to g8 without passing through f7, where a Black pawn stands, so this is impossible). The b-pawn would have had to make five captures to get to g8. The pawn now on f6 would in this case be the e-pawn, which would have needed one capture to get there. That's six captures. The a-pawn made one capture to get to b4. This scenario would have required a total of seven captures.

Now consider the e-pawn. For the e-pawn to have promoted on g8, it would have had to make two captures. In that case the pawn now on f6 would be the b-pawn, which would have needed four captures to get there. Adding the one capture needed by the a-pawn to get to b4, we again have a total of seven captures.

But since 10 of Black's original 16 pieces are still on the board, White could not have made seven captures. Therefore the promotion took place not on g8 but on some other square. As we've seen, that means that Black has lost the right to castle.

Now for the brilliant solution: White retracts 0-0-0 and plays 1 0-0-0! Black, unable to castle, has no defense against 2 dxc3 and 3 Rd8 mate (1 ... cxd2+ 2 Rxd2, etc.).

38. A: 1 Ra1 and 2 Ra8 mate (not 1 Rff7 hxg6). Black's last move had to be with either his king or rook and therefore he cannot defend by castling.

B: 1 Rff7 and 2 Rb8 mate. This time 1 Ra1? doesn't work because Black can castle. His last move did not have to be with his king or rook but could have been h7-h6.

39. 1 Qa1 and 2 Qh8 mate. Black cannot defend by castling because his last move must have been with his rook or king.

40. The last move was dxe6 e.p.+ after Black's e7-e5. It could not have been fxe6 e.p.+ because in the position with White's pawn on f5 and Black's on e7, Black is in check and White has no previous move. With the White pawn on d5, however, White's last move could have been (in fact it *must* have been) d4-d5+, which was followed by Black's e7-e5 and then White's dxe6 e.p.+.

41. Black must have moved his king, but it could not have come from b8 or b7, so it came from a7. On a7, however, it would have been in check by the White bishop. But the bishop could have arrived on g1 only from somewhere else on the same diagonal, meaning that Black would already have been in check. So the bishop did not move to g1 on the last move.

The only possibility is that a White piece moved off the bishop's diagonal creating a discovered check. But what was that White piece and what happened to it? It could only have been a knight and it's gone to horse heaven. The last White move was Nb6-a8 (or Nb6xa8) discovered check, to which Black replied Kxa8.

42. A nice try is 1 Bf7 mate, among others. But that assumes Black was the last to move. He couldn't have been, so it's his turn now: 1 ... Bxf6 mate.

43. Black's last move could not have been by his king, bishop, or either knight. So he must have moved his pawn, and it had to have moved from d7 because on d6 it would have been checking the king. White mates with 1 cxd6 e.p.

44. It was made by White, of course (Black has no last move), and it could only have been Kd1xNc1. No other Black piece could have been on c1: not a rook or a queen because it could have come to c1 only along the first rank and White could not have approached without being in check, and not a bishop because a bishop had no way to get to c1.

45. It must be Black's move, and he has no choice: 1 c6 b4 2 Ka3 Ra1 mate.

46. Sorry, the answer is not 1 0-0. By what route did the Black king reach a2? Only by crossing d2 and/or d1, which proves that at some point the White king was not on e1 guarding those squares. If White's king has moved, he can't castle. So: 1 Kf2 (not 1 Ke2 Nc3+) 1 ... N any 2 Qa1 mate. If 1 ... Ka1 then 2 Qxb1 mate.

47. White's last move was to transfer his knight from b4 to a2, capturing a bishop with check. If a2 had been unoccupied, Black would have had no previous move. The only piece that could have been on a2 was a bishop, which had to have moved there from b1. A knight could not have gotten there, and a rook or queen could not have moved there because the only access square was a1, where either piece would have been checking the White king.

48. Put the king on f3. White plays 1 0-0 mate. Why not put the king on c1 and play 1 0-0 mate? Because the king could not have reached c1 except by passing through d2 or d1. In that case the White king would have moved and he couldn't castle.

49. In both positions, the only legal squares for the White queen are to the left of the king and behind the pawn row, since without pawn moves the queen could not have left the first rank or moved to the other side of the king. In position A, placing the queen on e1 allows the move 1 f4 stalemate. In position B only two squares are available to the king's left. The correct one is a1, whereupon 1 a4 is stalemate.

50. The pre-castled positions of the White king and rook are meant to deceive. You probably see that placing the Black king on d3 allows 1 0-0-0 mate. That doesn't work, though, because then Black has no last move. But if it's Black's move in the diagram (who said it wasn't?), then put the king on d3 and play 1 ... Qg1 mate! If you insist that it's White's move, then put the king on c6 and play 1 Qb5 mate.

51. First, the Black king could not have just moved from a4 following White's a2xb3+ or b2-b3+ because in either case one of the bishops would have been impossibly located behind the pawns. The Black bishop did not make the last move either, since it could only have come from b2 where it would have been checking the king.

So the last move was White's, and it had to have been by the bishop. With the bishop on a2 and White to move, Black had no last move— unless he had another piece that the White bishop has just captured on b1. That piece could not have been a queen or bishop (how did it get there?). Could it have been a rook? In that case, Black's last move would have to have been Rb2-b1+. White's move before that would have to have been Bb1-a2. Black's move before that? There is none, since on a2 the rook would have been giving check.

Therefore, White's last move was BxNb1, and Black's previous move was Nc3-b1. Note that Black could not have played Nc3xb1 because, as we've already seen, there's no room in the corner for any additional pieces.

52. What was Black's last move? Analysis proves that it was f7-f5 and not d7-d5. The White pawns, to get where they are, had to have made 10 captures. Since there are still five Black pawns plus the king on the board, the White pawns took everything else: three Black pawns and the seven pieces except the king. That includes the bishop from c8. If Black's b-pawn and d-pawn had both been on their original squares, the bishop could not have left c8 and could not have been captured there by a pawn. Therefore, the d-pawn had previously advanced.

That leaves only the possibility of f7-f5. So the solution is 1 gxf6 e.p. and 2 f7 mate.

53. There are six Black men on the board. The 10 others have been captured. To get to their present positions the White pawns had to have made a total of five captures—one by the b-pawn, one by the c-pawn, and three by the e-pawn. If the bishop is a promoted pawn, it can only be the f-pawn, which would have needed five captures to reach a8 (via either a7 or b7). That's a total of 10 pawn captures. The g-pawn would have needed six captures to reach a8, which adds up to the impossible total of 11 captures.

Now consider the square f8, where once stood a Black bishop. Since the pawns on e7 and g7 prevented that bishop from moving, it must have been captured right there by a White piece. It could not have been captured by a pawn with Black pawns still on e7 and g7. And if White pawns did not make all 10 captures—which they clearly did not, as proved by the missing Black bishop—then there was no pawn on a8, and the bishop on a8 is not a promoted pawn.

The only way this position could have arisen is for the king to have moved from f3, setting up a discovered check by the bishop. But the king could have been on f3 only if it was shielded from the rook. The only possible scenario stems from the following diagram, showing the position a few moves earlier:

After 1 g4 fxg3 e.p.+ 2 Kxg3+ we have the position of the first diagram.

54. A: Does Black have a previous move? Yes! It was Ka7-a8 after White played b7-b8=B+. With White to move, the mate is 1 Ra7+! Kxb8 2 Nc6 mate.

B: This time there is no previous move for Black, so it is Black's move now: After ... Kxh7 there follows 1 Nf6+ Kh8 2 Rg8 mate.

A beautiful little twin miniature. Did you notice that White plays the same two moves in both positions but in reverse order?

55. Since Black's last move could not have been by a bishop, it must have been a pawn promotion on either g1 or h1. There could not have been a pawn on h2, however, because in that case the Black pawn position could have arisen only as a result of 15 pawn captures—but White is missing only 14 pieces! Check out that little White pawn hiding on a2!

So Black had a pawn on g2 before the last move. Was that move a capture on h1, promoting that pawn to a bishop?

Counting pawn captures, you will see that Black's g-pawn made one capture to get to h6, the f-pawn made two captures to get to h5, the e-pawn made three captures to get to h4, and the d-pawn made four captures to get to h3. That's 10 captures. The pawn on g2 could not have been the b-pawn because it would have needed to make five captures to get there, and White still has two pieces. So it must have been the c-pawn, which advanced one square and then made four captures. That's 14 captures in all. Capturing on h1 would therefore have been Black's 15th capture, which is impossible.

So Black's last move was g2-g1=B discovered mate!

56. Look at the rook on d4. If it's White's original queen rook, then the guy on a1 is the transplanted king rook, which means White can't castle because his king and rooks have moved. If it's the king rook on d4, then White had to have moved his king to let it out, and again he can't castle.

So let's say it's a promoted pawn. That rook, when it was a newborn babe, could have left the eighth rank only via d8, f8, or h8. In any of those cases, Black would have moved his rook or king and so *he* can't castle.

White plays 1 0-0-0! (2 Rd8 mate comes next). By castling, he demonstrates that his rook on d4 is a promoted pawn, which, as we have seen, deprives Black of the right to castle. If White plays 1 Rad1 instead, he is saying that although he may have the right to castle, he chooses not to exercise it. When Black plays 1 ... 0-0, he demonstrates that the rook on d4 is not a promoted pawn and that therefore White did *not* have the right to castle.

In situations where either side may claim the right to castle but the two claims are mutually exclusive, the convention is that whoever asserts the claim first has that right, which makes it illegal for the other side.

57. If Black made the last move, it could only have been the pawn advance g7-g6. But with the pawn on g7, the White king could not have reached h8. So the last move was made by White.

The knight? That piece could have appeared on f8 only by a pawn capture and promotion (g7xf8=N). But that is ruled out because with a White pawn on g7 before the capture/promotion, Black had no previous move (retro-stalemate).

The king? The last move could not have been Kg7-h8 because Black had no previous move. And not Kg8-h8 because that would have left g7-g6 as Black's only possible previous move, which, as we've seen, would have barred White's king from h8.

The last move could not have been Kg8xRh8 or Kg7xRh8 because a rook on h8 would have had no previous move. It could not have been Kg8xBh8 because the dark-square bishop is alive and well on d8. If it occurs to you that the bishop is a promoted pawn, observe that all the Black pawns are still on the board. The last move could not have been KxNh8 because, again, Black would have had no last move.

The only remaining possibility is Kg8xQh8.

58. Well, it depends. Let's say White plays 1 Ke6, threatening 1 Rd8 mate. Black castles and White has no mate. By castling, Black proves that his last move must have been g7-g5. But if White knows that Black has the right to castle, then he doesn't play 1 Ke6 but instead mates in two starting with 1 hxg6.

"Oh no you don't!" says Black. "My last move was Rh7-h8, not g7-g5, and you can't capture en passant."

"Have it your way," says White. "If you can't castle, I play 1 Ke6."

"In that case," says Black ...

Round and round she goes, and where she stops nobody knows.

What was *really* Black's last move? If a position has a history, it can have only a single history, and Black would not be able to choose what his last move was any more than I can choose today what I had for dinner last night.

This is not a real game, however, but a problem in chess logic. The position's history does not exist in actuality but only as a logical construct.

Sam Loyd once commented, probably facetiously: "Every composer knows that in making a problem the pieces are not *moved* into position, they are merely *placed*, and there has been no *previous* play." If that were really the case, of course, the retractor problem and all those treasures of retrograde analysis would not exist.

59. A: 1 d1=R a8=Q 2 Rf1 Qg2 mate. The Black king cannot move off the f-file because to do so would illegally check the White king!

B: 1 d1=B a8=N 2 Bb3 Nb6 mate. Again, the king can't move without giving an illegal check. All four promotions in one miniature!

60. 1 f6 (threatening Qf5 mate). Any move by Black to avoid checkmate illegally checks the White king. If 1 … Qc8 2 Nxd6 mate; or if 1 … Qxf6 2 Nc5 mate; or if 1 … d5 to close the h1-a8 diagonal, then 2 Qe5 mate.

61. 1 Ne8 threatening 2 Nc7 mate. Now 1 … Qf4 2 Kc2 mate (2 … Bxd1+ and 2 … Qd2+ are both illegal), or 1 … Qg3 2 Kc3 mate, or, best of all, 1 … Qd7 2 Re5 mate!! The unprotected rook can't be taken because Kxe5 is an illegal check! Don't you just love it?

62. The wrong tries are interesting. 1 R6c4+ or 1 R3c4+ is met by 1 … N6xc4 mate (the move 2 Rxc4 is check but not mate). The solution is 1 Qd6 Bxc6 (if 1 … Rxc3 2 Qe5 mate, or 1 … Nxd5 2 Rc4 mate because 2 … Nxc4+ is illegal) 2 Qb4 mate! Black can't interpose a knight (2 … N6c4+ or 2 … N3c4+) or capture the queen (2 … axb4+) because any of those moves is an illegal check!

63. 1 Kb7. Black's only move is to promote the c-pawn, and White answers 2 Rxc1 mate. Whatever the promoted piece is, it will not check White's king when it's replaced on the board (a promoted bishop would have to be put on the dark square f8). If White had moved his king to, say, b6, Black would have promoted 1 … c1=Q, and since 2 Rxc2 would return the queen to d1 where it would check the White king, the capture would have been illegal. You can easily see that b7 is the only square for the White king that allows White to capture legally on c1.

64. 1 Nf1 threatening Ne3 mate. A White rook can be taken in five different ways, but they all lead to mate after the rook is revived on h1. If 1 … Rxc2 2 Ng3 mate. If 1 … Bxc2 2 Ng3 mate. If 1 … Bxe2 2 Ne3 mate. If 1 … Nxc2 2 Re1 mate! (Black can't take the rook because when it's replaced on a1 it gives check). If 1 … Nxe2 2 Ne3 mate.

65. Black moves first: 1 c5 b4 2 cxb4 (the White pawn is returned to its original square, b2) 2 … bxc3 (the Black pawn comes back to life on c7) 3 bxc3 (the White pawn is resuscitated on c2) 3 … Ne3 mate. Did you notice that the two Black pawns changed places?

66. Parentheses indicate replacements: 1 Kc1 exd3 (Nb1) 2 Nd2 Kc3 3 Nc2 stalemate. Why can't Black play 3 … dxc2? Because replacing the knight on b1 would be an illegal check! The position after the solution is exactly the same as the starting position but transposed one square southwest.

67. 1 e4 Nf6 2 Qf3 Nxe4 (the pawn is replaced on e2) 3 Qf6 Nxf6 (the queen goes to g8!) 4 Kd1 Nxg8 (queen to e1).

68. 1 a5 h6 (or h5) 2 axh6 (e.p.) mate.

69. If it were Black's move right now, any move he made would be met by R4h5 mate. Here's the beauty of cylindrical chess. White plays 1 Rh4!, moving the rook completely around the cylinder, resulting in the same position but with Black to move.

70. It appears White has just delivered mate with the pawn on c4 and therefore should certainly not resign. Wrong.

To reach c4 the White pawn had to have just moved from d3 to make a capture, and to get to d3 in the first place it had to have made another capture in the past. But since Black is missing only one man, that is impossible.

The only way this position could have arisen is if Black was in the middle of playing d4(b4)xc3 en passant but has not yet removed the captured White pawn. As soon as he does, of course, White, not Black, stands mated. Since this is a cylindrical board, the rook on h5 is pinned by the queen on g6 along the diagonal g6-h5-a4-b3, preventing White from playing Rxd5.

The bottom line: Yes, White should resign (when Black completes his en passant move).

Postscript: The composer tells me that the answer is really No, on the grounds that it is bad manners to resign before one's opponent has finished moving.

Post-postscript: A little birdie tells me that since checkmate ends the game, resigning is beside the point.

71. 1 Rb2 Bxb2 (forced) 2 Rh8 Bxh8 (forced) 3 e4, and on the next move White will play 4 e5 forcing 4 ... Bxe5 and White wins. If 3 ... Be5, White wins by stalemate. The order of moves is important. If 1 Rh8? first, then 1 ... Bxh8 2 Rb2 Bxb2 3 e4 Bc1! and Black wins after 4 e5 Bh6 5 e6 Bg7 6 e7 Bf8, or 3 ... Ba3 4 e5 Bd6.

72. A: 1 f8=R is an elementary win (not 1 f8=Q?? stalemate).

B: 1 Kh6! forces 1 ... Kxh6 and then 2 f8=R! (not 2 f8=Q?? Kg7 and Black wins) 2 ... Kh5 (if 2 ... Kh7 3 Rh8; if 2 ... Kg7 or Kg6 or Kg5 3 Rf7 or Rf6 or Rf5) 3 Rf7 Kh4 4 Rf6 Kh3 5 Rf5 Kh2 6 Rf4 Kh1 7 Rf3 and wins. Note that 3 Rf6 loses after 3 ... Kh6 or Kg6 and White is forced to capture the king.

73. 1 Kb1 unguards the bishop on b3 so that 1 ... Rxd5 can be answered by 2 Bxd5 mate. If 1 ... Rc4, the unguarded knight mates with 2 Nb6 mate. If 1 ... Rxb4, the pinned bishop does not guard the knight, which mates by 2 Nc7.

74. 1 Qf8/Ke7 Qh6/Qxf8 2 Ke6/Kf5! and, regardless of Black's reply, White will capture Black's king on his next turn.

75. White plays either 1 Qd7+ or 1 Qe6+, one of which must be accepted. After 1 Qd7+ White refuses 1 ... Ke5, or after 1 Qe6+ White refuses 1 ... Kxe6, in either case forcing Black to play 1 ... Kc5. White then plays 2 Qc6 mate or, if that is refused, 1 b4 mate. Black has only one legal move, which White naturally refuses!

76. 1 Rc3. If 1 ... Qe1 2 R2c2 mate. If 1 ... Qd1+ 2 Rd2 mate. If 1 ... Qh1+ 2 Rg2 mate. If 1 ... Qf5+ 2 Ke5! mate. If 1 ... Qd3+ 2 Kd4! mate. If 1 ... Qe4+ 2 Kxe4 mate.

77. 1 Ba4 Ke5 2 Kc5 f3 3 Be8 Kf4 4 Kd4 Kxg5 5 Ke5 Kh6 6 Kf4 Kh7 7 Kg5 Kg8 (or Kh8) 8 Bg6 mate.

78. 1 Ka1 e2 2 Bb2 mate. The Black king can't go to any of the adjacent white squares because they're all controlled by White's bishop on a2 (e.g., the square g6 is attacked by the bishop bouncing from a2 to b1). And of course any adjacent black square is attacked in the same way by the bishop on b2. If 1 ... Ke5 2 Bg7 mate.

79. 1 Bb6 (If1), which is not check because 2 Bxa7 (I??) is illegal. Black has four moves.

If 1 ... Nc3 (Id2) 2 Kb4 (Ie1) and now the check to the Black king is unanswerable.

If 1 ... Nf4 (Ig3) 2 Kb5 (Ih3), with the same result.

If 1 ... Ng3 (Ih2) 2 Ka4 (Ih1), and again the check is unanswerable.

If 1 ... Nd4 (Ie3) and now no move by the White king works, but White has the retreating mate 2 Bxd4 (Ig1), an amazing move never seen in ordinary chess, and Black has no answer.

80. This somewhat mind-boggling problem begins with the key move 1 Rf7. Black has four replies, each answered by a different mating promotion.

If 1 ... Kxb6 2 c8=N double check and mate, but not 2 c8=B because the neutral bishop checks the White king(!), and not 2 c8=R because

Black uses the neutral rook to kill the check with 2 ... Rxd8 or 2 ... Rc7.

If 1 ... Nd7 2 c8=B mate, but not 2 c8=Q+ because Black simply moves the checking queen away along the c-file.

If 1 ... Ne6 then White does play 2 c8=Q mate (the king is also being checked by the rook) but not 2 c8=B+ because 2 ... Bd7 kills both checks.

If 1 ... Nh7 the moves 2 c8=Q+ and 2 c8=B+ are illegal because they check the White king, but since the knight move gives up control of the seventh rank, 2 c8=R is mate.

81. Play 1 ... d6 for Black, then remove the pieces on the following squares (in this general order, but some transpositions are possible): c6, e6, d5, b5, f5, e4, c4, d3, g3, g2, e1, d2, d1, b3, g4, h6, a3, e3, f4, b2, h7, f6, c3, d8, h8, b4, a8, d6, f8, b7, b6, and f7.

82. 1 Qb6. Since this temporarily immobilizes the queen, there is no stalemate. 1 ... K any 2 Kg1, which frees the queen to move again. Now the Black king is in check, and since it can't move (because it moved the last time), it is checkmated.

83. The answer is yes but, amazingly, only if White doesn't know precisely where the Black king is! For instance, he may know that it is somewhere on the last two ranks, in which case 1 g8=Q would be mate even though White can't pinpoint the king's exact location. The king can't be on the fifth or sixth rank, where it would already be in check. The only other square it could be on is a3, in which case White would know that precisely! His last move would have been a check announced by the umpire, and there's no other square to which the king could have moved.

84. If you try to set up the position on the board you will run out of Black pawns, since you need nine of them! To solve the problem, remove any Black pawn. For each one you remove, there's a different mate:

a-pawn: Qb6 mate
b-pawn: Nc6 mate
c-pawn: Qb4 mate
d-pawn: Qe4 mate
e-pawn: Bxf2 mate
f2-pawn: Bxe3 mate
f7-pawn: Ne6 mate
g-pawn: Rg4 mate
h-pawn: Rh4 mate

85. The position is illegal! The group of White pawns at the lower right is not possible, and neither is the group of Black pawns at the upper left. To solve the problem, legalize the position. Start by removing any one of those three Black pawns and make White's first move; then remove any of those three White pawns and make Black's first move; finally, make White's second move to deliver mate.

1. Remove the pawn on a6 and play 1 Nxa7 (keeps the b-pawn blocked); or remove the pawn on a7 and play 1 Na5 (keeps both queenside pawns blocked); or remove the pawn on b7 and play 1 Ba5 (keeps the a-pawns blocked).

2. Remove the pawn on g2 and now 1 ... Kxh3 2 Rxh5 mate; or remove the pawn on h2 and now 1 ... Kg5 2 h4 mate; or remove the pawn on h3 and now 1 ... Kg5 2 h4 mate. Black's replies are forced because the queenside pawns can't move.

86. White had given Black odds and was playing without his queen rook. He now "castles" with the "ghost" of that rook, claiming that when he gave up the rook he wasn't also giving up the right to castle: 1 0-0-0 (Kc1), and wins easily.

It seems strange to modern eyes, but the idea isn't really so far-fetched. In medieval chess, a king could make a two-square move once per game—the ancestor of castling.

In the next game, by the way, the loser got his revenge. See the next problem.

87. 1 Bh8!, "capturing" the phantom rook on a8 so that Black can't castle on the kingside! If 1 Rb7 planning 2 Rb8 mate, then 1 ... 0-0!!??, but not 1 ... 0-0-0??!! 2 Rb8 mate. Now comes 1 ... Ba2 (1 ... Kf8 2 Rd8 mate) 2 Be5 Bb1 3 Rb7 0-0-0!!?? (castling with the phantom rook on the other side, but it doesn't help) 4 Rb8 mate.

88. Black's last move could only have been b7-b5, to which White replies 1 cxb6 e.p.+, moving his pawn to b6 but not removing the Black pawn from b5, which would allow Black the defense 1 ... Rxb6.

89. 1 e8=R! Kg2 (or Kg1) 2 0-0-0-0-0-0 mate! That is, the king moves two squares toward the rook, and the rook moves to the other side of the king, as usual. (The notation represents the squares the rook passes over: two squares for 0-0, three squares for 0-0-0, and six squares for 0-0-0-0-0-0.)

Once upon a time, the official Laws of Chess gave the rules of castling in something like the following terms (paraphrased): The king

108

moves two squares toward the rook and the rook moves to the adjacent square on the other side of the king. Neither the king nor the rook may have previously moved, the king must not be in check, and the squares the king passes over and lands on must not be attacked by an enemy man.

All that applies to this position, does it not? The rook on e8, just now born on the board, has never moved.

But this castling is illegal, of course. The reason is that the *modern* Laws of Chess state (again I paraphrase) that the king and rook must be *on the same rank*. Such trifles as legality have never stood in the way of imaginative problem composers with a perverse sense of humor.

John Beasley's problem is an improved setting of this theme by Jean-Luc Seret in 1971. All the pieces in the Beasley position participate in the mate (if Black plays Kg2), whereas in the Seret setting the White king and bishop on h3 do not.

Jean-Luc Seret, Europe-Echecs, 1971

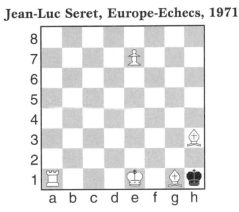

White mates in 2

Solution: 1 e8=R Kxg1 2 0-0-0-0-0-0 mate!

90. The amazing answer is 3 0-0-0-0-0-0 (king to e3, rook to e2) mate! All three castlings in a single problem.

91. Vertical castling is a feature of several mate problems, but this is the only endgame study I've seen with that move.

1 e6 a3 2 e7 Kb1

If 2 ... Kb2? 3 e8=Q wins; e.g. 3 ... a2 4 Qe2+ Kb1 5 Kd1! a1=Q 6 Qc2 mate.

3 e8=R!!

After 3 e8=Q? a2, White can neither stop Black from promoting nor make progress in the queen endgame, and exchanging queens with 4 Kd2 a1=Q 5 Qe1+ Kb2 6 Qxa1+ Kxa1 7 Ke3 leaves White a tempo short of winning the pawn endgame.

3 ... a2 4 0-0-0-0-0-0!?!

That is, king to e3 and rook to e2. Bringing the king to e3 in one move instead of two (4 Kd2 and 7 Ke3) gains the tempo necessary to win; e.g., 4 ... a1=Q 5 Re1+ Kb2 6 Rxa1 Kxa1 7 Kd4 and wins.

92. 1 h2 Nc3 2 h1=White rook! 0-0 mate!

93. Despite all that heavy White material, a mate in two is not to be found. If 1 Kg1? not 1 ... Kxg3? 2 Qf2 mate, but 1 ... h2+!

Remember that Sam Loyd joke (see solution number 58): The pieces are placed, not moved, and there has been no previous play. That's the only way to justify this solution: 1 0-0!! and 2 Qe2 mate. If there has been no previous play, as Loyd claimed, then neither the king nor the rook has previously moved and castling is therefore legal according to the rules! Call your lawyer if you want.

94. Note the words "any piece." Put a *Black king* on b8 and play 1 Qc6. Black is stalemated.

95. This is an illegal position because there is no way for the Black king to have legally arrived at a2. Black, probably thinking he could pull a fast one, must have put it there while White wasn't looking. Saying "None of *that*, my friend," White picks up the Black king, puts it on any legal square, and mates in one.

96. Lift the White king and look again! See, I told you there was a mate. Don't put it down again, or you'll spoil it.

97. If this puzzle mystifies you, you're probably assuming that White is moving up the board. Simply rotate the board 180° and *voilà!* Does that count as a move?

98. It would be nice if White could play 1 0-0 mate, but unfortunately he's in no position to do that. If you look closely, you'll see that the square h1 is black, which means that it isn't h1 at all but actually h8. So turn the board 90° counterclockwise and make the correct move: 1 e8=N mate! Why can't the dark square in the corner be a1 instead of h8? Because then the pawn would be on d2 giving an impossible check.

99. The only possibility is 1 g8=Black knight!

100. The clever attempt 1 e8=Black knight, threatening 2 f8=N mate, doesn't work because of 1 ... Ng7! (not 1 ... Nxd6 or Nxf6 because of 2 Nc5 or Bf5 mate). Correct is 1 e8=Black bishop!! (threatening 2 f8=N mate) 1 ... Bd7 or Bxf7 2 Re5 or Qf5 mate.

101 A: 1 f8=Black bishop! and 2 Nf7 mate.
  B: 1 fxg8=Black rook! and 2 Nf7 mate.
A delicious miniature.

102. If 1 exf8=Black rook+? Be7! 2 Kxc7 stalemate (2 Bg4? Ng5 and 3 ... Bxe6 wins for Black).
  If 1 exf8=Black bishop+? Bfe7! 2 Nd7 stalemate.
  If 1 exf8=Black knight+? Nxe6! 2 fxe6 f5 and White doesn't have enough to win.
  So 1 exf8=Black queen+! Qe7 2 Nd7 (2 Rxe7+? Kxe7 and wins) Qxe6+ 3 fxe6 Ke7 (if 3 ... Be7 4 Kxc7 Bd8+ 5 Kc6 and wins after 6 Nf5 or 6 Nxe4 with a mating net) 4 Nf5+ Kxe6 (if 4 ... Ke8 5 h3 and 6 Kxc7) 5 Bg4 Ng5 (5 ... Be7 6 Ng7 mate) 6 Nc5+ Kf7 7 Bh5+ Kf8 8 Nd7 mate.
  After 1 exf8=Black queen+, if 1 ... Be7 2 Kxc7 Qg7 3 Nxe4 (threatening 4 Nd6+ Kf8 5 Nd7 mate) 3 ... Qg5 4 Nd6+ Kf8 5 Nd7+ Kg7 6 Ne8 mate.

103. 1 g8=Black queen! Qg7+ 2 fxg7 c2 3 g8=Q c1=Q 4 Qxf7+ Kd8 5 Qe8+ Kc7 6 Qc8+ Kb6 (6 ... Kd6 7 Qc5+) 7 Qc6+ Ka7 or Ka5 8 Qb7 or Qb5 and draws. White's queen is then taken for stalemate.

104. 1 d8=king! and now 1 ... Kc6 (or e6) 2 Rb2 (or f2) Kd6 3 Rb6 (or f6) mate.

105. 1 e8=Black king! relieves the stalemate. When that king moves to d8 (as it must), White mates both kings with 2 Qd7!

106. A: 1 d8=king!
  B: 1 d8=*Black* king!!

107. White is in check, and his only reasonable move is to capture on f8 (1 Qg8? Qxg8 mate). But 1 exf8=R allows stalemate after 1 ... Qg7+ because the new rook guards the d8 square after 2 Bxg7. Similarly, 1 exf8=N guards d7 allowing 1 ... Qh7+ and stalemate, and 1 exf8=Q or B guards d6 allowing 1 ... Qg8+ and stalemate.

111

The answer is 1 exf8=pawn! Since the pawn is on the eighth rank and can't move, it is what problemists call a dummy pawn. Now 1 ... Qg7+ 2 Bxg7 releases d8, or 1 ... Qh7+ 2 Bxh7 releases d7, or 1 ... Qg8+ 2 Qxg8 releases d6, or 1 ... Qxf6+ destroys the stalemate at once and White will win after Black gives a few checks to stay alive a little longer.

108. 1 Kh8 Kd2 2 g8=P! Re1 3 g7 Re6 (trying to avoid stalemate by giving White a move) 4 dxe6 Rb1 5 e7 b2 6 e8=P!! Qxg8+ 7 hxg8=P!!! and 8 h7 with stalemate.

109. Obviously, 1 a8=Q (or any White piece) leaves Black stalemated. Promoting to a Black piece is no help; for instance, 1 a8=Black knight Nc7! and there is no mate (but not 1 ... Nb6 2 Rc5 mate). As Sherlock Holmes said: When you have eliminated the impossible, whatever remains, however improbable, must be the truth. So: 1 a8=neutral knight! This knight functions as either a White knight or a Black one and can be captured by either side. Now if 1 ... Nb6 2 N2c4 mate (the knight can't be taken because Black would be checking his own king!), or 1 ... Nc7 2 N3c4 mate (the king can't go to b5 because the knight on c7 guards that square).

110. White is in check, and he has no practical choice (Qf8 or Qd8 is met by RxQ mate) but to promote the g-pawn. But to what? Certainly not to a queen, rook, bishop, or knight, since 1 ... Bxf6+ ends the game. But this creaky old chess club still uses its original wooden chess sets. White craftily selects a knight with a loose base and plays 1 g8=N. When Black plays 1 ... Bxf6+, White picks up the knight—that is, its loose head—and captures the bishop with it, leaving the base of the knight on g8 to protect the king. If 1 ... Rxg8+ instead, then of course White is perfectly safe after 2 Kxg8.

111. If you figure out the answer, please let the author know immediately.

A Crash Course on Chess

You're marooned on a desert island and the only thing you've managed to save is this book of interesting-looking chess problems. But you can't solve them because you don't know how to play chess!

Or you've picked up this book of interesting-looking chess problems in a bookstore because of the provocative cover, but as you leaf through it you find the puzzles totally mysterious: you don't know how to play chess!

Or, worse, you're trapped at the mother of all boring parties and the only book you can find in the host's home is this collection of interesting-looking chess problems. But even this offers only frustration: you don't know how to play chess!

Help is here. Below is a quick-and-dirty summary of the greatest of all games—enough to give you a rudimentary knowledge of the mechanics (not the strategy) of orthodox chess: the setup, the moves and relative values of the pieces, the rules, the basic checkmates. Although many of the problems in this book are not orthodox, you still need to know the rules so you can recognize when they're being bent or broken.

The Board

The chessboard consists of 64 alternating dark and light squares in what is jocularly known as a checkerboard pattern (why don't they ever call it a chessboard pattern?). The game is a battle between two armies of contrasting light and dark colors, which are always called White and Black. They begin the battle facing each other at opposite ends of the board. When set up for play, the square at the White player's right hand must be white. Remember: white on the right.

The columns of squares leading from the White side to the Black side are files. The rows running across the board from left to right are ranks. The diagonals are diagonals. To record games and positions, the "algebraic" system of chess notation is used: The files are assigned the letters a through h beginning at White's left, the ranks are numbered 1 through 8 beginning at the White side of the board, and the conjunction of letters and numbers gives each square its unique name (see Algebraic Notation, page 14).

The Opening Setup

Each player's army consists of 16 men comprising eight pieces— one king, one queen, two rooks, two bishops, and two knights— and eight pawns. The pieces are set up facing each other on the first and eighth ranks: king facing king, queen facing queen, etc., as shown in the diagram. The queen always begins on its own color. Remember: White on white, Black on black. The pawns are set up in front of the pieces, on each player's second rank.

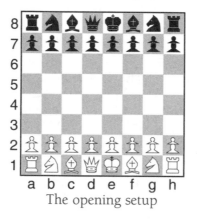

The opening setup

The Object of the Game

The game is won by defeating the enemy king. When a king is attacked ("checked") and cannot escape or parry the attack, it is checkmated. This ends the game at once. Check and checkmate are described more fully below.

Checkmate is rare in games between good players. Usually, one player obtains such a large advantage that the opponent resigns in recognition of the inevitable.

A game can also end in a draw, which is a win for neither side. The several kinds of draws are explained below.

How the Pieces Move

A move consists of transferring a single man from one place to another (castling, however, which I'll tell you about later,

114

involves moving two men). Every move must be made either to a vacant square or to a square occupied by an enemy man. In the latter case, the enemy man is captured and removed from the game, and its square is taken over by its captor. Except for the knight, there is no jumping. Capturing is not compulsory unless there's no other move. The king is never captured.

Pieces move along straight, unobstructed horizontal, vertical, or diagonal lines. The knight combines horizontal and vertical movement. Pawn moves are explained below.

The king moves one square horizontally, vertically, or diagonally. It may not move to a square attacked by an enemy man.

The queen moves any distance horizontally, vertically, or diagonally.

The rook moves any distance horizontally or vertically.

The bishop moves any distance diagonally. Each bishop is restricted to the color it starts on. The bishops on f1 and c8 in the setup diagram above may travel only on the light squares, the bishops on c1 and f8 may travel only on the dark squares, and never the twain shall meet.

The knight combines two directions in an L-shaped move: two squares vertically or horizontally and one square at a right angle; or vice versa. The knight always moves a distance of two squares to a square of the opposite color. It is the only piece that can jump over or move around other men.

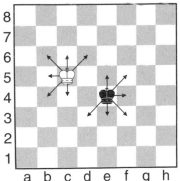

The moves of the king. The two kings cannot
approach each other because each king controls, or
"attacks," the squares next to it.

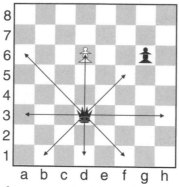

The moves of the queen. In this position, it can capture the White pawn but can't pass the Black one.

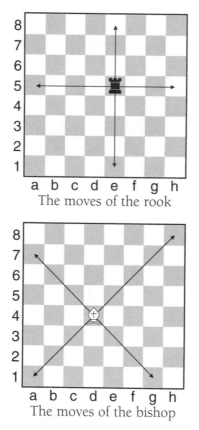

The moves of the rook

The moves of the bishop

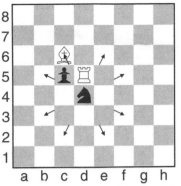

The moves of the knight. It is not blocked by other men and can capture the bishop on c6.

How the Pawns Move

The basic pawn move is one square straight ahead. But pawns have several special attributes.

Each pawn, on its first move only, may advance either one or two squares. Thereafter, however, it may advance only one square.

Although pieces capture the same way they move, pawns don't. A pawn captures one square diagonally forward. If the square directly in front of a pawn is occupied, it can't advance. But if a square diagonally in front of it is occupied by an enemy man, the pawn can capture it.

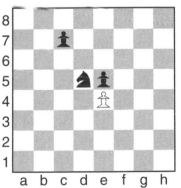

The Black pawn on c7 may advance to c6 or c5.
The White pawn on e4 can't advance because it's blocked by the Black pawn on e5, but it can capture the Black knight on d5.

Pawns have another special capturing power. If a pawn is on its fifth rank, and an enemy pawn on a neighboring file tries to pass it by advancing two squares on its first move, that pawn can be captured as if it had advanced only a single square. This maneuver is called en passant, a French term that means "in passing." An en passant capture applies only when the neighboring pawn has advanced two squares on its first move, and it may be carried out only on the very first opportunity, not later.

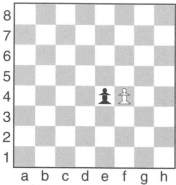

The White pawn on f4 has just advanced two squares, trying to pass the Black pawn on e4.

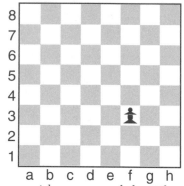

The Black pawn on e4 has captured the White pawn en passant by moving diagonally to f3, as if the White pawn had advanced only one square. The White pawn is out of the game.

Pawn Promotion

When a pawn reaches the last rank, it's promoted to any other piece of its own color (except a king). The promoted piece assumes its new powers at once. Because it's usually promoted to a queen, the most powerful piece, this move is often called queening. A promoted pawn may become any piece regardless of how many pieces of the same kind the player already has. Since each pawn has but one life to give for its cause, a player can't have more than eight promoted pieces. In theory a player can have, for instance, nine queens (the original plus eight promotions), but in practice it's rare to see more than one promotion in a competitive game, though multiple promotions are common in endgame studies.

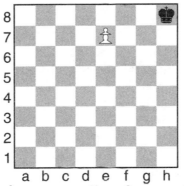

White advances the pawn on e7 to e8, promoting it to a queen.

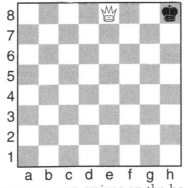

The moment the new queen arrives on the board, it attacks the enemy king.

Castling

Since defeating the king is the focus of the enemy's operations, chess provides a means to allow it to move to a safer spot than the middle of the board where it starts out. This maneuver is called castling, which each player may perform only once. The king moves two squares toward a rook on the same rank, and that rook moves to the adjacent square on the other side of the king. A player may castle either "short" or "long." Short castling is on the "kingside," the half of the board where the king begins the game; long castling is on the "queenside," the half of the board where the queen begins the game. In orthodox chess, castling is permitted only under the following conditions:

•The king may not be in check, though it may have been previously checked.

•The king or rook may not have previously moved.

•The squares between the king and the rook must be unoccupied.

•The squares the king crosses and lands on may not be under enemy attack. This does not apply to the rook.

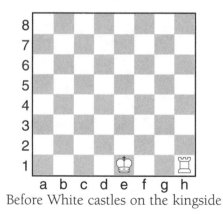

Before White castles on the kingside

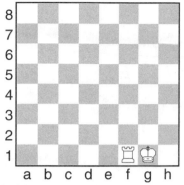

White has castled by moving the king two square to the right
and the rook to the other side of the king

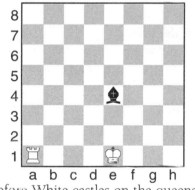

Before White castles on the queenside

White has castled by moving the king two squares to the left and the rook to the other side of the king. The rook may cross square b1 even though that square is attacked by the enemy bishop.

Relative Values of the Pieces

As a general rule, and other things being equal, the player with the stronger army will win. The strength of an army is measured not only by the number of men it has but by the values of those men compared with the values of the enemy's.

The value of a piece is based on its mobility in most positions. The queen, because it can travel any distance in any of eight directions, is the most mobile and therefore the most valuable piece. But very often the relative values of the pieces are less important than positional considerations. For instance, a pawn that can't be prevented from promoting is as strong as a queen. A bishop that is blocked and can't move is worth less than a knight that can jump over anything in its way.

The relative values are important because they help players decide whether an exchange of captures is favorable or not. A player who recklessly exchanges his valuable pieces for the enemy's less valuable ones is likely to end up with a dead king.

Opinions vary, but the most commonly accepted values are:

Pawn: 1
Knight: 3
Bishop: 3+
Rook: 5
Queen: 9

The king has no value when calculating exchanges because it can't be captured. It's nominally valued at 5 because it is a strong piece in the endgame, when there are few pieces on the board and it is not in danger of being checkmated.

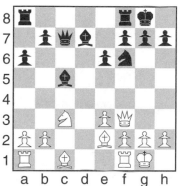
White takes the Black knight with his queen

But Black can then capture the queen with a pawn. The result: White has lost a queen (9 points) in exchange for a knight (3 points)—a bad deal for White in this position.

Check and Checkmate
The object of the game is to checkmate the enemy king. When a king is attacked, it is in check. Although the king is never actually captured, the imminent threat of unavoidable capture—checkmate—ends the game.

A king is required to get out of check immediately. Check may be parried in several ways:

• By capturing the checking piece.
• By interposing a man between the checking piece and the king.
• By moving the king to a safe square.

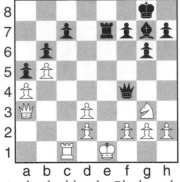

The White king is checked by the Black rook. White can either capture the rook with his queen, interpose his knight at e2 or e4 between the rook and his king, or move his king to d1 or f1.

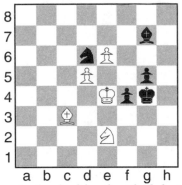

The White king is checked by the Black knight. The knight can't be captured and no piece can be interposed, but the king can move to d3, the only available square that is not under attack. It can't move to d4 or e5, which are attacked by the Black bishop, or to e3, which is attacked by the Black pawn on f4, or to f3, f4, or f5, which are all attacked by Black men.

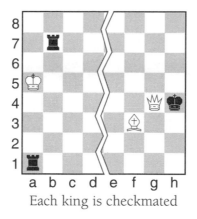
Each king is checkmated

Stalemate and Other Draws

If the king can't get out of check, it is checkmated. If it's *not* in check but neither it nor any of its men can make a legal move, it is stalemated. This is a draw, and neither side wins.

It's Black's move. His king is not in check, but because he has no legal moves, he is stalemated and the game is a draw.

A game can be drawn in other ways. The most common is by agreement: When neither side believes he can improve his position enough to win, the two players may agree to abandon the game and call it a draw.

The Laws of Chess decree that a game is drawn "by repetition" when the same position is about to be reached for the third time with the same player to move. This is often a sequence of repeated checks ("perpetual check") that neither player can afford to stop because the alternative is worse.

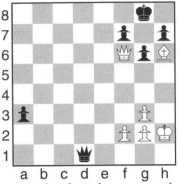

Neither side can avoid a draw by perpetual check. If it were White's move, he would play Qg7 checkmate. The only way Black can prevent that is to perpetually check the White king by moving his queen back and forth between h5 and d1. If White interposes his queen on h4 after Black gives check on h5, Black will take the queen and then advance his pawn to a2, winning easily after the pawn is promoted.

A game can be drawn due to "insufficient mating material." If each player has a king only, neither can win. If one player has only a king plus a knight or a bishop (no pawns), and the other side has only a king (no pawns), the extra piece is not enough to win: it is impossible to set up a checkmate position. An extra rook or queen can win, however. Even a single pawn is enough to win because it can be promoted to a queen!

Index of Constructors

Numbers refer to problems.

About the Author

Burt Hochberg is the author of *Title Chess: The 1972 U.S. Chess Championship* (1972), *Winning With Chess Psychology* (with Pal Benko, 1991), *The 64-Square Looking Glass: The Great Game of Chess in World Literature* (1993), *Mensa Guide to Chess* (2003), *Sit & Solve Chess Problems* (2004), and *Award-Winning Chess Problems* (2005). He was the editor-in-chief of *Chess Life* magazine for 13 years, senior editor (now editor emeritus) of *Games* magazine, Executive Director of the Manhattan Chess Club, Executive Editor of R.H.M. Press, and the author of the major articles on chess and electronic games for the Microsoft Encarta Encyclopedia. He received the "Outstanding Career Achievement" award by the U.S. Chess Federation and the Fred Cramer award as "Best Chess Book Editor" (both 1996). He has been a columnist for ChessCafe.com, and his articles have been anthologized in various journals. In 2004 he was a primary inductee to the new Gallery of Distinguished Chess Journalists. He lives with his wife, Carol, in New York City.